S0-BTA-751

Container WATER GARDENING *for hobbyists*

Container WATER GARDENING for hobbyists

From the Publisher of *Aquascape Lifestyles* Magazine

Publisher & Editor-In-Chief............ *Greg Wittstock*

Consumer Publications Editor............ *Tamara Hughes*

Marketing Communications Manager............ *Jennifer Zuri*

Graphic Design Service............ *Icon Digital Design & Illustration, Inc.*

Creative Director............ *Mike Stout*

Senior Art Director............ *Colleen Hughes*

Staff Photographers............ *Tony Alcala, Matt Stout*

Contributors............

Writing............
Kelly Clancy, Tamara Hughes, Oscar Warmerdam, Rick Weidman, Jennifer Zuri

Photography............
Marieke Den Das, Scott Hughes, Rick Weidman, Jim Wullschlegger

Illustrations............ *Daria Corbett*

Container Water Gardens............
Tony Alcala, Ed and Ellen Beaulieu, Gared Bell, Chris and Laurie Beytes, Rick Byers, Daria Corbett, Jet Dekker, Conor Doyle, Julie Griffin, Kathy Haben, Dave Havrilka, Colleen Hughes, Tamara and Scott Hughes, Dave Kelly, Michelle Kurschner, Diana Opelia, Inga Orolin, Tavia Tawney, Cyril Wochok, Jennifer Zuri

Container Water Gardening for Hobbyists

ISBN # 0-9786506-5-4
is published by the Pond Guy™ Publications

A division of Aquascape, Inc.
P.O. Box 638, West Chicago, IL 60186
www.aquascapeinc.com
www.aquascapelifestyles.com

Printed in the U.S.A.

Table of

CONTENTS

Chapter 1

GETTING STARTED

ALL THE RIGHT INGREDIENTS

Recipe for Container Water Gardens

1 part love of gardening

2 parts love of water

A dash of creativity

A pinch of imagination

Mix together in a barrel, bowl, tub, or other receptacle and enjoy a gorgeous container water garden that was invented by the best designer in the world ... YOU!

This is the recipe for the perfect water garden – a water garden that can be moved from one spot to another...from the backyard, to the front yard, from one side of the patio to the other. This is also a recipe for a hobby enjoyed by people of all ages, young and old. Anyone who ever thought being a water gardener strictly involved a large, water-filled hole in the backyard has never been captured by the beauty and simplicity of a container water garden.

WHAT IS A CONTAINER WATER GARDEN?

Perhaps the recipe listed on the previous page didn't go into enough detail about the components involved in the creation of a container water garden. Any vessel that holds water and supports plant life can be considered a container water garden. There are a lot of reasons to have a container water garden, ranging from space restrictions to accenting the backyard and garden.

> *Some people believe that having a container water garden can add personality to their garden. Surrounded by gorgeous perennials, they are considered a pleasant surprise when passersby see or hear the water.*

Those with limited space can tuck a container garden virtually anywhere since they come in all shapes and sizes. Some people believe that having a container water garden can add personality to their garden. Surrounded by gorgeous perennials, they are considered a pleasant surprise when passersby see or hear the water.

The truth is, there isn't any single, clear reason why you should have a container water garden. In fact, we should point out that container water gardens aren't always a replacement for a large water feature. Many full-fledged pond owners dot the rest of their landscapes with container water gardens because of their mobility and ease of maintenance. They also can be used to accent the current pond and provide a balance in the landscape.

Surrounding your container water garden with beautiful perennials creates a nice focal point in your backyard.

BABY STEPS

A container water garden is a great first step when considering whether or not you'd like an in-ground water feature in the future. If you're worried that you won't be able to grow aquatic plants, this can be a great way to get your feet wet with water gardening. Getting a large pond installed without any water gardening experience can be intimidating, so container water gardening is a good introduction to a fascinating and exciting hobby.

OH THE PLACES THEY'LL GO!

When it comes to the location of a container water garden, the sky is the limit. If you really start to consider your surroundings, you could think of five or six places right off the top of your head in which to put these gardens. The common spot would be on the deck or patio ... a beautiful focal point while you're grilling outside with friends or relaxing after a long day of work.

Have you ever thought, however, about having your water garden greet visitors at the front door? Instead of the common welcome mat, your friends and family can be invited in by the plants and gurgling water in your unique container. Many times, people are so focused on what their backyard looks like that they forget about the curb appeal of a nice container in the front yard.

Spicing up a perennial garden is always a good choice when it comes to the placement of your container garden. You could consider a green container to blend into the garden or choose a bright color that would make the leaves and flowers pop out. This change in color and texture will make any perennial garden stand out from the rest.

Or maybe you want to be different and put it on the side of your house, or in the corner of your vegetable garden. Anywhere that pleases your senses is the way to go when deciding on the perfect spot for your container. Best of all, if you don't like it, you can move it!

The deck or patio is a beautiful focal point while you're grilling outside with friends or relaxing after a long day of work.

Indoor tabletop containers are a great way to showcase your container water garden.

WHICH KIND WILL YOU CHOOSE?

There's a container water garden for every taste, style, and place. They range from the more traditional kinds to the downright funky styles and every container garden certainly isn't the same. A lot of it comes down to your tastes. Do you want a tall, thin container, a short stubby container, or perhaps an out-of-the-ordinary shape that defines your lifestyle?

There are a few things you need to consider when deciding on the type of your container water garden. Will it have a pump keeping the water aerated and perhaps feeding a small fountainhead or spitter? Or would you like your water to be serene and still like a calm pond in the middle of a forest? Maybe you'd like to see some water flow outside the container, but aren't quite sure where the water would go. The answer is a catch basin that would simply re-circulate the water back to the pump, but you may need a little more room for this plan.

You may not have decided whether you'd like your container water garden to be inside or outside, but a tabletop garden could be on your radar. There are some great varieties of indoor and outdoor tabletop containers that would provide a great focal point and conversation piece. And what a way to set yourself apart from the neighbors!

Yet another decision the potential container water gardener has to make is what will go into the pot. Will it simply be water, or will you add a little soil or polished stones to complete the look? Does your idea of the perfect water garden include some finned friends? Will your container water garden be overflowing with many plants or will it elegantly feature one focal plant?

THE ANSWER

You're the only one that can answer all these questions because the style, location, and contents of your water garden is up to you. We can, however, give you some great ideas and step-by-step processes to help you through the building process. We'll walk you through materials, such as what kinds of containers, pumps, and decorative accents to use, and then we'll show you how to put them all together.

We'll introduce you to some aquatic plants that work well in containers, as well as the critters that could call your water garden home. And we'll even fill you in on what kind of upkeep you can expect with your water garden. Hopefully, you'll use this book as you create your container water garden because it has everything you need to make a decision on your design. Of course, there is one piece missing that you'll have to find...your inner water gardener!

Will your container garden simply be water, or will you add a little soil or polished stones to complete the look?

Chapter 2

MATERIALS

AND CONSTRUCTION

Container water gardens range from a simple container of water with a single, floating water hyacinth to an elaborate set up of pumps, plumbing, plants, and fountains, and almost anything in between.

The materials you'll need to build your container water garden will depend on the complexity of your project. Be informed about the items you may need and how they are used to create your own little corner of aquatic serenity.

THE CONTAINER

The most important element for your container water garden is the container itself. The possibilities of what you can use are almost endless. From the simplicity of terra cotta, to a fancy cast iron urn, or a treasure you found in the garage, to a glossy ceramic pot, you are only limited by your imagination.

The color and type of container you choose will dictate the style of your container water garden. Some containers are quite striking and don't need a lot of embellishment. On the other hand, a plain container will provide a simple foundation for more dramatic plants. If you're not sure where to start, thumb through the pages of this book to get ideas for your own container water garden.

Don't limit your container selection to something you purchased. You may have something around the house that would make a unique container for aquatic plants.

When it comes to the shape and size of the container, keep in mind where it will be located. A short squatty pot might look lost tucked in a group of towering cannas, but take that same pot and place it in front of its taller counterpart and you'll appreciate the visual depth you just created for your landscape.

What about that old cooler you have sitting in your garage?

TYPES OF CONTAINERS: *The possibilities are endless!*

Metal Urn

Watering Can

Terra Cotta Pot

Coal Bucket

Bowl

Ceramic Pot

Terra Cotta Pot

Milk Pail

Wooden Wash Basin

Oblong Metal Container

On the other hand, a tall pot with a strong presence might look awkward and out of place in a tiny corner of a patio, but place it next to the front entrance of your home, and it makes a dramatic, yet welcoming statement to your guests and visitors.

YOU MAY ALREADY HAVE THE PERFECT CONTAINER

Don't limit your container selection to something you purchased. You may have something around the house that would make a unique container for aquatic plants. What about that old coal bucket or the milk pail you got from your grandparents' farm? Or that old washtub that you bought at the flea market?

And when bigger is better, even an old clawfoot tub can look striking with aquatic plants when placed in an area of the garden that needs visual interest. Tie the tub into the landscape by planting flowers or a small shrub into the nearby soil. Anything you find that has the ability to hold water can be the container that holds your new water garden. The possibilities are endless.

KEEPING IT CONTAINED

Whatever type of container you decide to use, it's important to make sure that it will hold water. Most glazed ceramic pots are water-tight, however it's possible that you will encounter a drainage hole at the bottom. There are a number of ways to plug the hole and how you go about it often depends on the size of the hole. Rubber plugs or corks work well along with a bead of silicone sealant around the perimeter of the plug. Another option is plumber's putty. Use it to plug the hole and once it is in place, add a bead of silicone sealant around the edges to keep any water from leaking out.

Some garden centers are now carrying what they call "aquatic bowls." These containers are usually made of plastic or ceramic that is glazed inside and out, and without holes.

If the pot you have chosen is made of porous material such as terra cotta or unglazed ceramic, you will also need to seal the inside of the container to prevent water from leaching out. Simply coat the interior of the pot with a waterproofing product like concrete sealer.

Some garden centers are now carrying what they call "aquatic bowls." These containers are usually made of plastic or ceramic that is glazed inside and out, and without holes. You may also find flexible, plastic liners without drainage holes that fit inside various size pots. This is yet another option for making your container water-tight.

GARDEN TIP:

It is often recommended that you use dark colored containers when building a container water garden because it will disguise the growth of algae along the inside walls of the container. While this is true, it will limit your options. See Chapter 5 for tips on preventing algae growth in your container water garden.

KEEPING IT WATER TIGHT

Coat the interior of the pot with a waterproofing product...

Or use a plastic liner...

Or simply plug the hole with a rubber plug, a cork, or plumber's putty.

TYPES OF FOUNTAIN HEADS

COMMON PUMP USES

75 gph – Among the smallest of the statuary and fountain pumps, this one works well for most container water garden sizes when a slight amount of water movement is desired at the surface. Also good for some smaller sizes of fountain heads and spitters.

145 gph – This pump works well for larger container water gardens when a slight amount of water movement is desired at the surface. Can also be used on small to medium size fountain heads and spitters.

210 gph – You need a little more power to push water through the smaller sized resin and brass spitters. This pump will do the trick in most cases.

350-500 gph – Use a pump in this size range for medium to large stone statuary or brass spitters, 24 inches or more tall. A higher gph is required to pump water to the top of taller fountains or spitters.

PUMPS, SPITTERS, AND FOUNTAINS

Now that you've found the perfect container and picked the perfect spot for it, the next important item to consider is the addition of a pump, spitter, or fountain.

A pump can be placed in the container to create a bubbling effect on the water's surface if you prefer a subtle effect, or you can add an extension or plastic tubing to the pump, to which a fountain head can be connected. Either effect will add the subtle sound of water movement.

CHOOSING THE FOUNTAIN

The length of the tubing or extension will be determined by the depth of your pot. Different fountain attachments produce different shapes the water takes when spraying, so choose a spray type and size that works with the size and shape of your pot to avoid overspray outside the pot. You should also consider the selection of plants you're using by avoiding a fountain with a large spray diameter that will knock over the plants in your miniature water garden.

Smaller pumps, like these 145 and 210 gph statuary pumps, are perfect for small fountains and bubblers commonly added to container water gardens.

You can experiment with the length of hose attached to the pump to help control the height of the fountain spray, and make sure the gallons per hour (gph) of the pump is appropriate for the size and type of fountain. The garden center employee can help with this selection however; the pump's packaging will include the number of gallons per hour the pump can handle.

ADD CHARACTER WITH A SPITTER

If you prefer something a little more decorative than a fountain head, you can opt to add a spitter to the pump. Spitters come in an assortment of materials, shapes, and sizes. Resin spitters are lightweight and generally inexpensive, making an economical choice. They're available in the form of fish, frogs, turtles, flowers and more. In addition, some resin spitters can be quite colorful. But once again, consider the color and size of your container, in addition to your plant selection, when choosing a decorative resin spitter.

For a classic, traditional look, consider a brass spitter. Although a little higher in price than resin spitters, they are a worthy investment because they're long-lasting and, over time, develop a beautiful patina. Like resin spitters, you can find brass spitters in a variety of shapes and sizes, from pineapples, to fish, to flowers. Brass spitters look great in both rustic and contemporary containers.

NICE BUT NOT NECESSARY

Pumps, spitters, and fountains aren't necessary elements for a container water garden. You may want to avoid using pumps or spitters so the focus of the garden remains solely on the quiet beauty of the aquatic plants. While pumps, spitters, and fountains play a vital role in aerating the water, they are not a requirement for a healthy container water garden.

Brass Spitter

Resin Spitter

Container water gardens can be as simple as one floating plant in a bowl.

Plants will thrive in a container water garden without aeration, but if you choose to go this route, be sure to add a larvicide or some fish to keep mosquito larvae from developing (see Chapter 5 for more details). If you don't have easy access to outdoor electricity for running a pump, then a simple container with aquatic plants is the way to go.

Plants will thrive in a container water garden without aeration, but if you choose to go this route, be sure to add a larvicide or some fish to keep mosquito larvae from developing.

ON THE LEVEL

When planting your containers, it's important to pay attention to the planting depth listed on the plant's care tag. While some aquatics like water lilies are submerged underwater and can generally be placed at the bottom of your container,

GETTING A LIFT

Using a scrap of plastic milk carton-like material, cut to just the right size, can do the trick for many containers. And the holes mean you can place the pump below it and still be able to easily string the cord up and out of the container. There are also products on the market meant to be used in a traditional container garden, to lessen the amount of soil needed, that would work to create a platform for your aquatic plants.

Using bricks...

a plant saucer...

a plant pot tipped upside down...

or create your own heightened device.

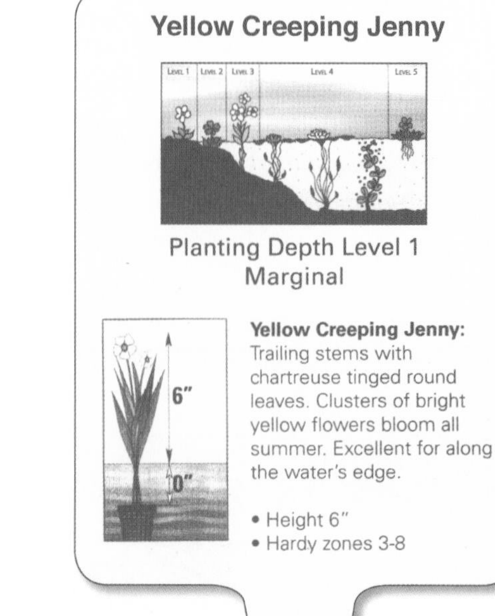

Plant tags will tell you which water depth your plant requires.

many marginal plants prefer to grow right at or slightly under the water surface. To do this, some plants will need to be raised within the container so they are closer to the surface of the water and therefore planted at a shallower depth.

This can be done by adding any number of items or materials to the bottom of the pot. Flat stones or bricks can be stacked to the appropriate level and, due to their small size, can be staggered to accommodate the depth of different plants. Pots turned upside-down and set inside the decorative container can sometimes do the trick as well. Another trick is to use a saucer that would normally be placed under a pot, inside the decorative pot with the correct measurement to lock it into place at the right level for the plants to sit on. Unfortunately, there isn't one perfect way to do this. It all depends on the size and shape of the container that you're using, so you may have to get creative to find the best solution. This can be the most challenging part of creating a container water garden.

ROCKS AND GRAVEL

Small rocks, river rock, and/or pea gravel are other materials you may want to have at hand when you're building your container water garden. You may opt to use them to build up the planting level inside your container. You could even fill the entire container with pebbles or river rock and plant the aquatic plants right into the gravel.

If you leave the aquatic plants in their original growing pot, you can cover the soil with pebbles or river rock to prevent the pot (and the plant) from floating, to cover the rim of the planting pots, or to simply decorate your container.

Larger rocks can be used as an accent within the container water garden and add a nice element to the whole look.

ROCK & GRAVEL OPTIONS

A. Use gravel to cover the soil to prevent the pot from floating. B. Use small rocks or gravel to build up your container garden or place your plants directly in it. C. Add larger rocks for a nice design element.

PLANTING POTS

If you are starting out with small plants that come in small pots, you may want to "bump up" the plant into a larger container. This means that you're simply re-potting your new plant into a larger pot. The benefit is a larger pot that is less likely to float, but mostly a larger pot gives the plant more room to grow which results in a bigger, healthier plant.

HANGING PLANT BASKETS

Be sure to check your local garden center for plant baskets that hook over the edge of a container so that no stacking is needed.

ADDING WHIMSY

Gardeners who appreciate a little whimsy or drama in their landscape can take the container water garden one artistic step further by adding goldfish, floating balls, glass gems, lights, and more to the container.

A small, floating glass ball adds visual interest to a simple container filled with water and floating plants like water lettuce. This type of container is easy to create, and provides a simple focal point in the landscape.

GARDEN TIP:

If you're a finicky gardener, you can go one step further in hiding any cords by drilling a hole near the bottom of your container for the cord to run out of so it's not spilling down the side of the pot. If you opt for this set-up, simply fill any gaps between the cord and the hole of the pot with plumber's putty and add your water sealant to prevent leakage. If you're drilling through ceramic or terra cotta, be sure to use a masonry bit to avoid cracking the container. Putting heavy tape over the hole before drilling helps prevent the drill bit from "wandering" across a slippery surface.

If you like to enjoy your garden in the evening, consider adding an underwater light or floating lily pad light to the container. You'll want to make sure you hide the light's cord so your miniature water garden doesn't become unsightly. If your container water garden is tucked into the corner of a patio, simply position any cords to run over the backside of the container. And if your miniature water garden is settled in the midst of a garden, you can strategically add plants near the container to

SOMETHING A LITTLE DIFFERENT

Another decorative water feature to consider adding to your garden is a bubbling urn or rock fountain. If you enjoy the sound of running water, but don't necessarily want to incorporate aquatic plants, you can convert almost any container into a refreshing, bubbling focal point. Water garden manufacturers have created sturdy basins that sink into the ground, acting as a reservoir for stand-alone fountains, spitters, or bubbling containers. The larger the basin, the less you'll need to add water throughout the gardening season.

You can purchase the basin at a garden center or from an installer, then dig a hole in your garden the same size as the basin, or have an installer do it for you. Carefully place the basin in the hole and follow manufacturer's guidelines for completing the installation. After placing the decorative piece on top of the basin, cover the rest of the basin top with decorative stone.

DRAMATIC OPTIONS

Several options are available when adding an aquatic basin with a decorative water feature to your garden and, as a general rule, you can change the decorative feature that sits on top of the basin, so your options are almost limitless.

For a quiet gurgle of running water, bubbling urns are a good choice to use with the basin. After the urn is placed atop the basin, you simply fill the reservoir with water and turn on the pump. The pump pushes the water up and over the edge of the urn, and the water falls back down into the basin to be recycled back through the urn.

Bubbling Urn

For a more dramatic water feature, columnar stones can be used with the basin. Garden centers and installers sell these in a variety of sizes, and they come manufactured with the hole already drilled through the center for easy hook-up to the pump.

If you prefer a little whimsy, there are a myriad of spitters available for use with the basin. Make sure that you choose a style that gently spits the water within the diameter of the basin. If the flow rate is too strong, the water will fall outside the basin and won't be circulated, which means the water in the basin will eventually disappear. Remember that the pump needs a continual water supply in order to function properly.

hide the cord as it descends from the top of the container. You can then bury the remainder of the cord into the ground and run it to the nearest electrical outlet.

MIX IT UP AND HAVE FUN!

You may not be ready for a full-fledged pond, or you may not have the space for one. That's why container water gardens allow anyone the opportunity to dabble in water gardening.

You can use just a few materials for the simple water garden, or you can choose to be more elaborate by adding fountains and decorative elements. Open your yard and imagination to the many creative possibilities afforded by container water gardening. Whatever your water feature choice, be sure to experiment with the wide variety of containers and decorative elements that lend themselves to this growing segment of gardening. Your choices for beautiful container water gardens are almost limitless.

Chapter 3

PROJECTS

STEP-BY-STEP INSTRUCTIONS

WARNING: The projects you see in this chapter are incredible. The process of building a container water garden can be addicting, and the urge can oftentimes get out of control. If proper measures aren't taken, you may fill your yard with beautiful container water gardens, with little to no room for a lawn. Completed container water gardens may cause serenity and bliss. Please proceed with caution.

Now that you have an idea of why you would want a container water garden and what kinds of materials to choose for your garden, it's time to take a look at how they are put together. Remember first that container water gardens can vary not only by their container, but by what goes into that container.

Will you choose a project that contains a pump? A pump marks the difference between moving water and still water, but whether you use a pump depends on where your water garden will be placed. If it's not next to an electrical source, you may have to go with a still and serene setting or find an interesting way to disguise your electrical hook-up.

If you have a pump, do you want the water to bubble gently, or do you prefer a spitter that shoots water in the air before finding its way back into the pot. And when the water reaches that pot, will it be greeted by rocks and gravel or a splash of water? Perhaps a combination of all will be perfect for your creation.

Will you choose a project that contains a pump? A pump marks the difference between moving water and still water, but whether you use a pump depends on where your water garden will be placed.

Do you have a green thumb, and are you capable of dipping it into the blue? The actual process of water gardening can be very rewarding, and the type of container water garden you choose may be dependant on what kinds of plants you want in your container.

With all of the options out there, it can be pretty overwhelming to build your own water garden. So why not peruse the following pages and check out some projects with step-by-step directions? With plants and without, with pumps and without... the options are all there! Maybe you'll fall in love with Cantaloupe Cabana or be inspired by Tea Time. Aqua Lime may give you the perfect direction for a container ripped right out of your imagination. For great ideas and the methods you need to make them a reality, turn the page!

FISH SPITTER

FOUNTAIN

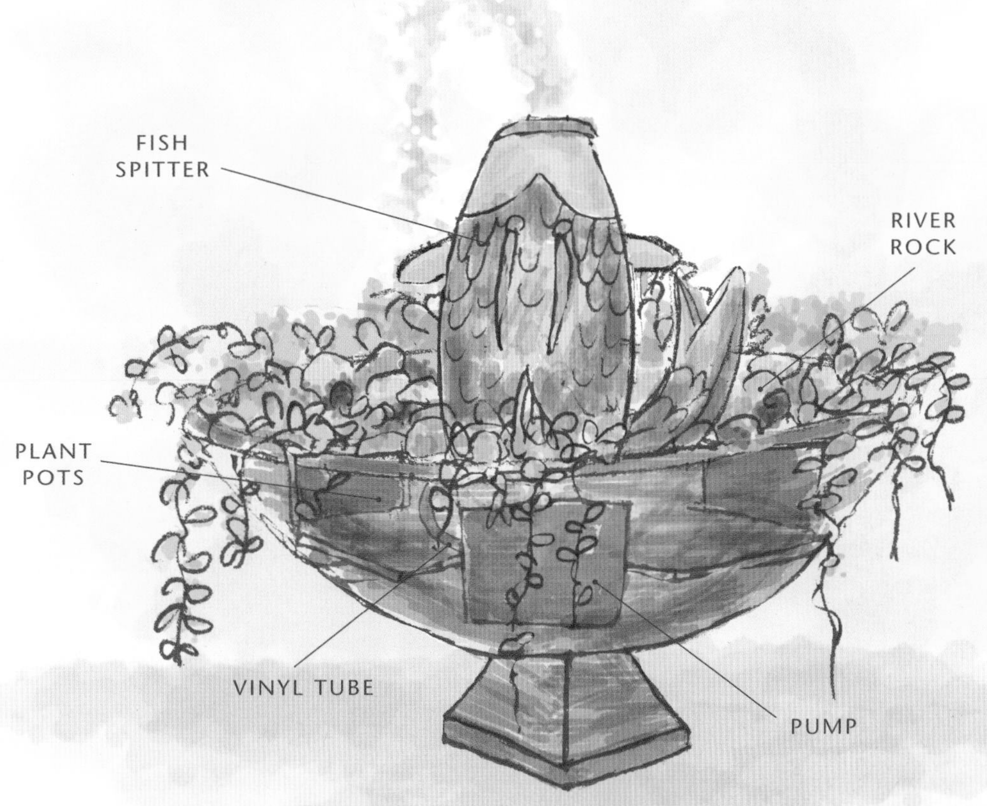

MATERIALS:

- 24-inch ceramic low bowl
- 500 gph statuary pump
- 1 to 3-inch river rock
- Brass fish spitter
- Milk crate-like grate
- ½-inch vinyl tubing

PLANTS:

Pennywort, Variegated (*Hydrocotyle sibthorpioides* 'Variegata')

TIPS:

Using a piece of milk crate-like grate to support the plants and fountain created a space below to house the pump. It also meant less rock was needed to fill the container.

PROJECT ONE

FISH SPITTER FOUNTAIN

STEP 1:
Collect all the materials.

Collect everything you'll need before you get started. This will ensure that the project is an enjoyable one without unnecessary trips to the store. Washing the rocks in a plant basket before adding them to your container water garden helps keep the water clean.

STEP 2:
Cut the grate.

Using a jigsaw or hand saw, cut the grate to size so it sits about 2 inches from the top of the container. Cut holes in the grate to accommodate the shape of the plants' growing containers.

STEP 3:
Hook up the pump and spitter.

Place the pump at the bottom of the container and connect the ½-inch vinyl tubing to the pump and the spitter. Cover the pump with the grate.

STEP 4:
Arrange the plants.

Arrange the plants into the pre-cut holes. You can use plants that are all the same type or you can mix them up and use different types.

STEP 5:

Arrange the rocks.

Arrange the rock so the grate is covered. If you'd like, you can add one or two larger rocks as a focal point in your container.

STEP 6:

Fill container with water and enjoy!

Now your container is ready to be filled with water.

FINAL

TEA TIME

FOUNTAIN

MATERIALS:

- Matching oval ceramic containers. One, 9 x 16 inches. Another, 14 x 24 inches
- 75 gph statuary pump
- Tea cup and pitcher to create fountain
- ½-inch vinyl tubing
- Moss
- Silicone
- Plumbers putty
- Pea gravel
- 2-inch river rock
- Aquatic plant pot

PLANTS:

Variegated Canna
(*Canna* 'Pretoria')

Dwarf Variegated Sweetflag
(*Acorus gramineus* 'Ogon')

Bloody Dock
(*Rumex sanguineus*)

Pitcher Plant
(*Sarracenia* 'Judith Hindle')

TIPS:

Positioning this dual container water garden on stone steps adds a little extra height to the upper container. Moss is a wonderful thing ... especially for hiding plant basket edges and naturalizing the whole look. Don't have any moss? Go for a walk in the woods!

PROJECT TWO TEA TIME FOUNTAIN

STEP 1:

Set the pots in place.

This is not the kind of container water garden that you can simply move around. You will need to place the pots on soil so the tube can exit the bottom without getting crushed,or set them on terraced outcropping stones. Situate the containers slightly off the edge so the tubing can come out the bottom. Level the pots so the water does not spill out one side.

STEP 2:

Set up the plumbing.

This container already had a hole at the bottom of the pot. After placing the pump in the bottom of the smaller container, attach the tubing to the pump and run it though the hole in the small pot, careful not to kink it. Continue running the tubing up through the hole in the large pot, leaving a long enough piece of tubing to connect to the tea pot later on.

STEP 3:

Seal the holes.

The tubing should fit snugly inside the holes. Fill any gaps with clear, silicone sealant. It's a good idea to use a generous amount inside as well as on the outside the pot. Follow manufacturer's instructions for drying time. Note: If your container doesn't already have a hole, you can run the tube over the edge of the pot but you will then need to hide it from view. A hole can also be drilled in the bottom or side of your container.

STEP 4:

Drill a hole in the tea pot.

To accept the ½-inch tube, drill a hole in the tea pot. To avoid cracking, apply duct tape on the inside of the tea pot where the hole will be drilled. Use a small (3/16-inch) masonry bit to drill a pilot hole. Then use a ½-inch bit for the final hole to accommodate the size of the tube.

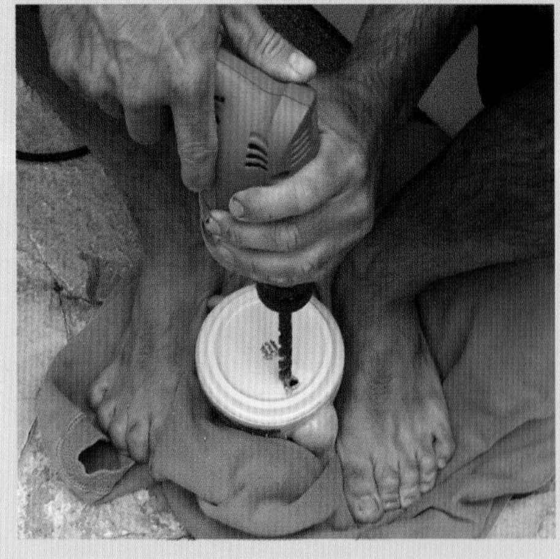

STEP 5:

Set up the tea pot.

Run the tubing through the hole that you drilled in the tea pot and seal around it with clear silicone. Cut the excess tube. For extra support, use a piece of stiff wire, like an un-folded clothes hanger. Then, place a walnut-size amount of plumber's putty on the lip of the pot where the tea pot will rest. This will help hold the tea pot in place.

STEP 6:
Attaching the tea cup.

Any found object – in this case, a plastic cup – can be used as a place to set the tea cup. An aquatic planting pot could also be used. If the item has no holes, add some so that it will not float. Use plumber's epoxy to attach the plastic cup to the bottom of the tea cup and hold it in place.

STEP 7:
Adding the rocks.

To access the pump more easily, put a plant basket upside down over it and surround with rock. Place the aquatic plants and decorate with rock and moss. Don't forget to add some small rock inside the tea cup.

STEP 8:
The finishing touches.

The final step is to add moss and plants.

FINAL

CANNA BOWL

MATERIALS:

- 16-inch round, low planting bowl
- 75 gph statuary pump
- Pea gravel

PLANTS:

Chinese Ground Orchid
(*Blethilla striata*)

Narrow-leaved Arrowhead
(*Sagitaria gramineus*)

Bloody Dock
(*Rumex sanguineus*)

Variegated Canna
(*Canna* 'Pretoria')

Water Hyacinth
(*Eichhornia crassipes*)

TIPS:

The water in this easy-to-build container water garden is kept clean by running a small statuary pump. The water movement circulates and oxygenates the water, which helps stave off excessive algae growth.

PROJECT THREE CANNA BOWL

STEP 1:
Add the pea gravel.
Fill the container part way with pea gravel.

STEP 2:
Planting time.
Remove the plants from their pots and place into the gravel.

STEP 3:
Fill in.
Add gravel around the base of the plants so they are stable.

STEP 4:
Add the pump.
If you are using a pump, this is the time it would be added to the container. Set it on top of the rocks so the outlet is just under the surface of the water.

STEP 5:
Add water.

Fill the container with water up to just under the lip of the pot.

STEP 6:
Enjoy!

Enjoy your low maintenance water feature and don't forget to keep the water topped off at the proper level.

FINAL

TURQUOISE URN

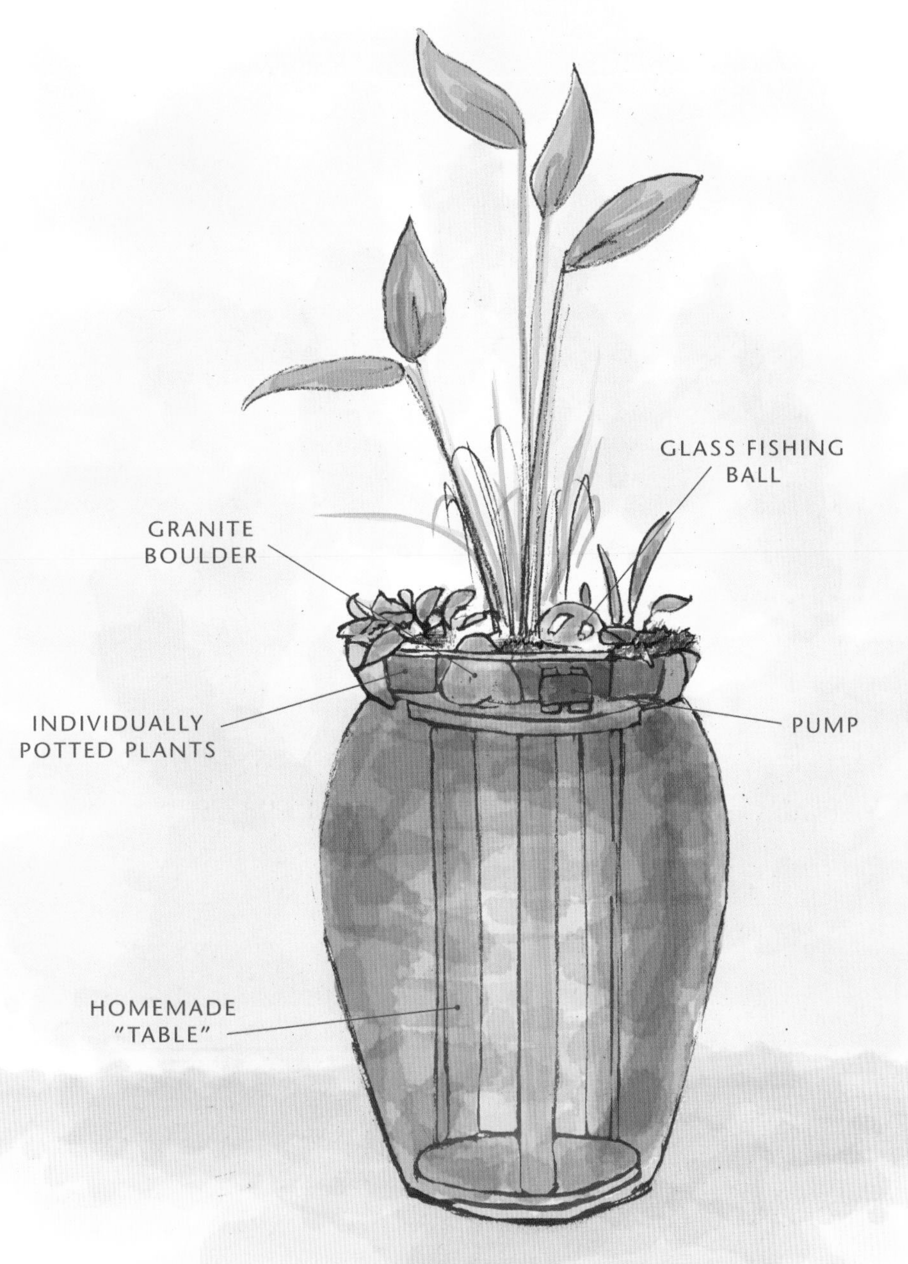

MATERIALS:

- Glazed ceramic urn, 18 inches diameter, 36 inches tall
- 75 gph statuary pump
- Treated plywood and 2x4s
- Pea gravel
- Medium granite boulder
- Glass fishing ball

PLANTS:

Red-Stemmed Thalia (*Thalia geniculata* 'Rumnoides')

Creeping Buttercup (*Ranunculus repens* 'Buttered Popcorn')

Black Magic Taro (*Colocasia esculenta* 'Black Magic')

Blue Water Forget-Me-Not (*Myosotis scorpoides*)

Parrots Feather (*Myriophyllum aquatica*)

Dwarf Variegated Sweetflag (*Acorus gramineus* 'Ogon')

TIPS:

A small granite boulder and a colorful glass fishing float add a nice touch to this container water garden.

PROJECT FOUR TURQUOISE URN

STEP 1:
Build a plant platform.

With a very large container that has an opening narrower than the widest part, you'll need to get creative to come up with a way to raise the planting level for the aquatic plants. Here, an elaborate table, constructed out of treated lumber, was created so it could be pieced together inside the container. You'll need to devise the best method of doing this for your container.

STEP 2:
Set it up.

Set up the platform inside the container.

A

B

STEP 3:
Add water.

Cover the platform with black fabric so the light color does not show after the container is planted. Fill the container with water.

STEP 4:
Cover the dirt.

Use pea gravel to cover the soil in the plants' growing pots. This will help keep the dirt from clouding the water.

STEP 5:
Installing the pump.

With some small pumps, it is possible for a little dirt in the water to clog the filter. In this case, the filter can be removed to improve water flow.

STEP 6:
Hide the pump.

Use the leaves of nearby plants to help hide the pump so it is not visible, while keeping it far enough away from them so you can still see and hear the water movement that it creates.

STEP 7:
Add whimsy.

Moss, a small granite boulder, and a glass fishing float all add a little whimsical interest to the container water garden and breaks up the flush of foliage that fills in as the plants grow.

FINAL

PROJECT FIVE

CANTALOUPE CABANA

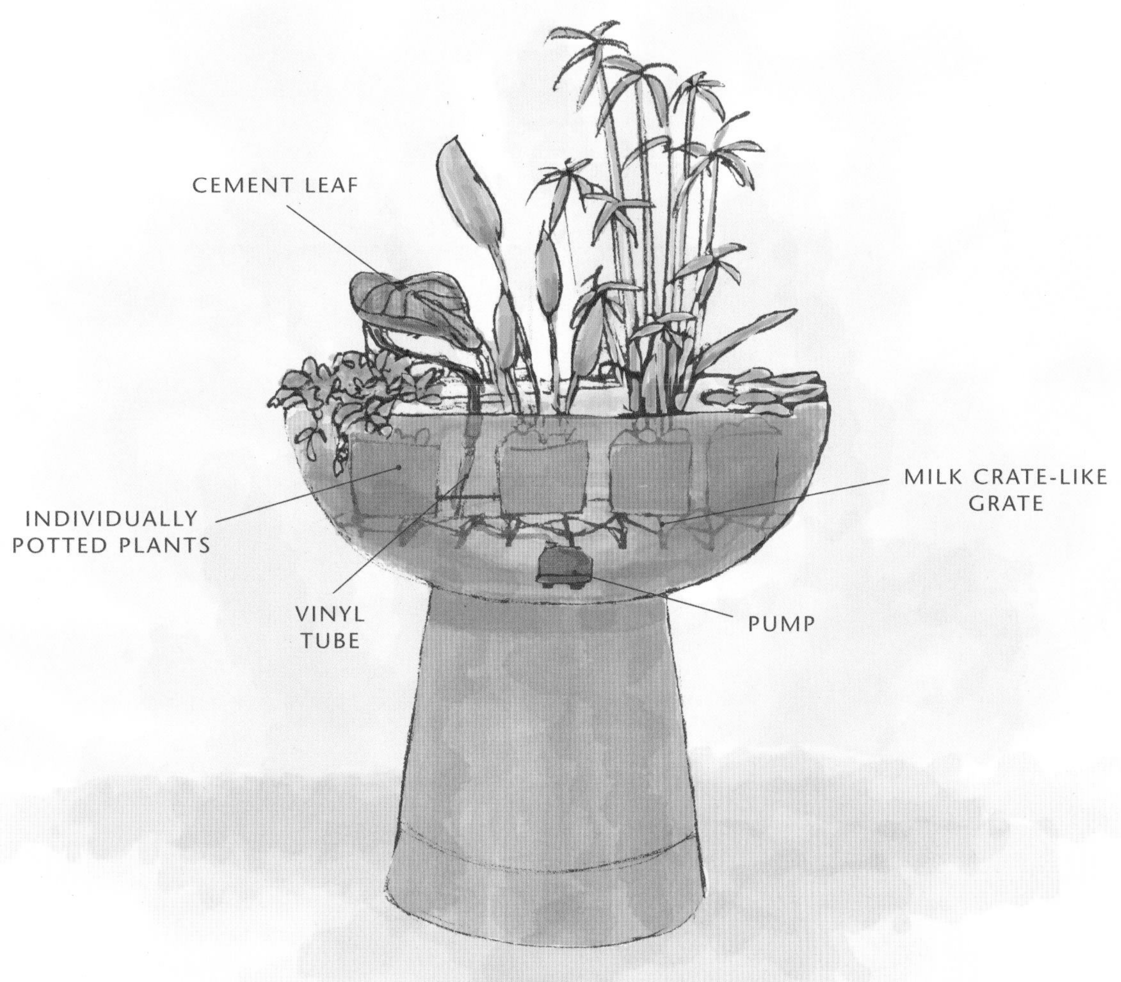

MATERIALS:

- 24-inch round ceramic pot
- 145 gph statuary pump
- Liner patch
- Silicon sealant
- Electrical tape
- Cement leaf
- ¼-inch vinyl tube
- stones
- ¼-inch 90-degree poly barbed fitting
- Wire plant stake
- Green bamboo stake

PLANTS:

Floating Heart (*Nymphoides peltata*)

Dwarf Umbrella Palm (*Cyperus alternifolius* 'Gracilis')

Silk Stockings (*Sagittaria australis*)

Creeping Buttercup (*Ranunculus repens* 'Buttered Popcorn')

Lemon Bacopa (*Bacopa caroliniana*)

Narrow-leaved Arrowhead (*Sagittaria gramineus*)

TIPS:

If you can't find a cement leaf, put your creative hat on and look at garden ornaments in a different way. You never know what you might come up with for your very own container water garden fountain.

PROJECT FIVE CANTALOUPE CABANA

STEP 1:

Collect all the materials.

Having everything on hand when you begin your project will ensure that it will be an enjoyable project rather than a frustrating one.

STEP 2:

Connect the fountain, plumbing, and electrical.

For support, the cement leaf rests on a heavy wire plant stake normally used for perennials, reinforced with a green, bamboo stake. Hook up the vinyl tubing to the statuary pump. To keep things neat, use electrical tape to secure the pump cord to the vinyl tubing. If your container has a hole, be sure to plug it so water does not leak out.

STEP 3:

Support the plants.

Cut the piece of milk crate-like grate to the appropriate size so it supports the plants at the correct level for their desired planting depth. Set the grate inside the container over the pump.

STEP 4:

Testing the water.

Before you fill the container all the way, just add enough water so the pump is submerged to allow you to test and adjust the water flow from the fountain. You should also check to be sure that your container is level. If it is not, you will be able to tell by the uneven water level.

STEP 5:

Planting time.

Arrange the plants to your liking, leaving some open (un-planted) water for the fountain to trickle back down and into the container.

FINAL

PROJECT SIX

BLUE MOON

FOUNTAIN

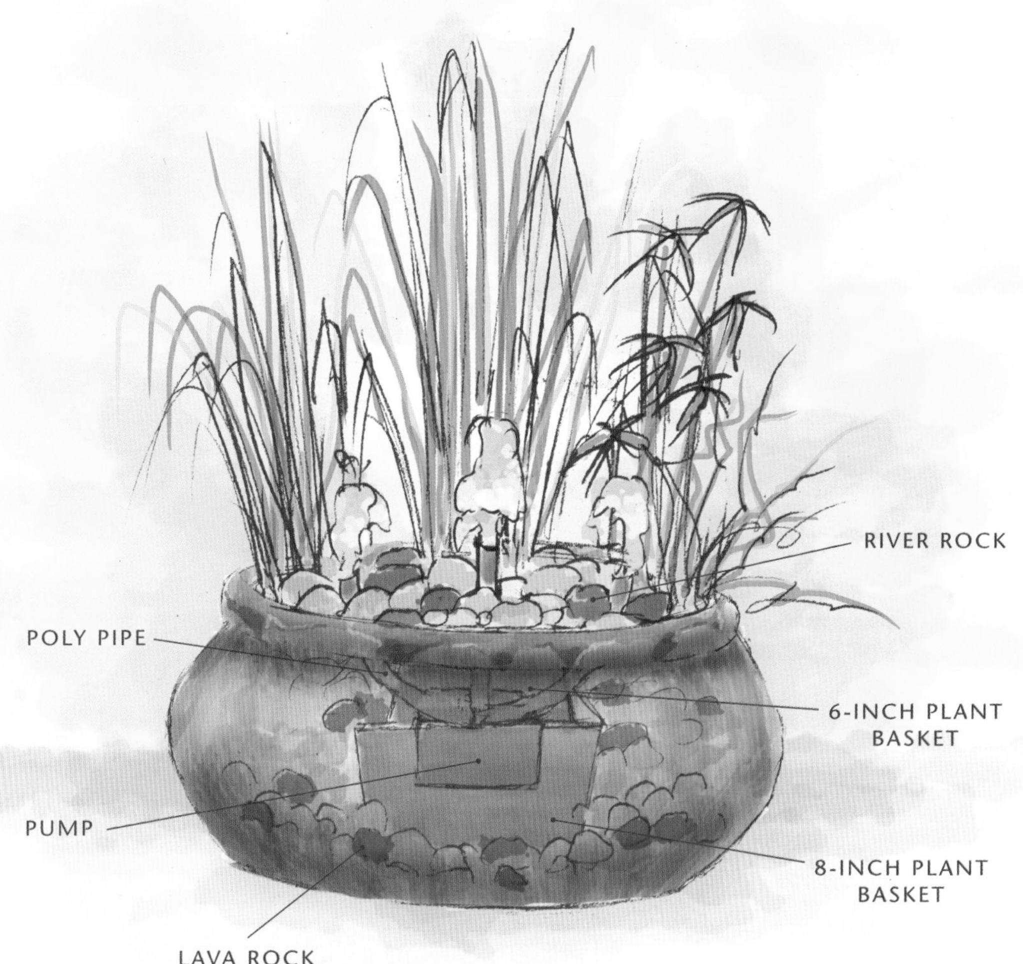

MATERIALS:

- 20-inch shallow ceramic water garden bowl
- 500 gph pump
- 6-inch square aquatic plant basket
- 8-inch square aquatic plant basket
- 1-inch poly, barbed, tee fitting
- 1-inch poly pipe
- Fountain divert valve
- Fountain telescoping extension
- 2 to 3-inch river rock
- Lava rock

PLANTS:

Sprial Rush
(*Juncus effuses* 'Spiralis')

Dwarf Variegated Sweetflag
(*Acorus gramineus* 'Ogon')

Common Rush
(*Juncus effuses*)

Miniature Umbrella Palm
(*Cyperus alternifolius* 'Gracilis')

TIPS:

Because this container was intended for use as a container water garden, there is no hole, eliminating the need to plug the drainage hole.

BLUE MOON FOUNTAIN

STEP 1:

Collect all the materials.

Having everything on hand when you begin your project will ensure that it will be an enjoyable project rather than a frustrating one.

STEP 2:

Place the pump.

Place the pump inside an aquatic plant basket for easier access once the container is built.

STEP 3:

Connect the plumbing.

Connect the divert valve and telescoping extension to the pump according to manufacturers instructions. Extend a short piece of 1-inch poly pipe and then connect that to a tee fitting. From there, add a 6-inch piece of 1-inch poly pipe to each end of the tee. These will later be part of the fountain.

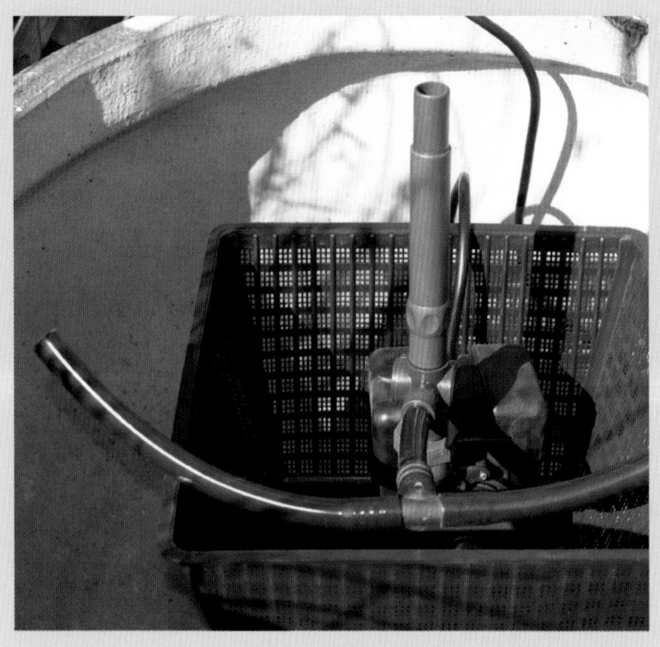

STEP 4:

Adding the rocks.

Fill the bottom half of the container with lava rock. Lava rock works well as a light weight and inexpensive filler.

STEP 5:
Cover the pump.

Cut a hole in the bottom center and on two sides of a 6-inch square plant basket. Place the basket upside down over the pump, positioned so the fountain diverter valve pokes through the hole on the bottom and the poly pipe sticks out the sides.

STEP 6:
Fill in with decorative rocks.

Add decorative rock up to the level where the aquatics will be planted.

STEP 7:
Time for the plants.

Arrange the plants in your container. This arrangement revolves around the placement of the fountains so they can be seen.

STEP 8:
The rest of the rocks.

Fill the remainder of the space with rock so the pump and the plant baskets are covered. Trim the poly pipe so it is just an inch or so above the surface of the rock.

FINAL

PROJECT SEVEN

AQUA LIME

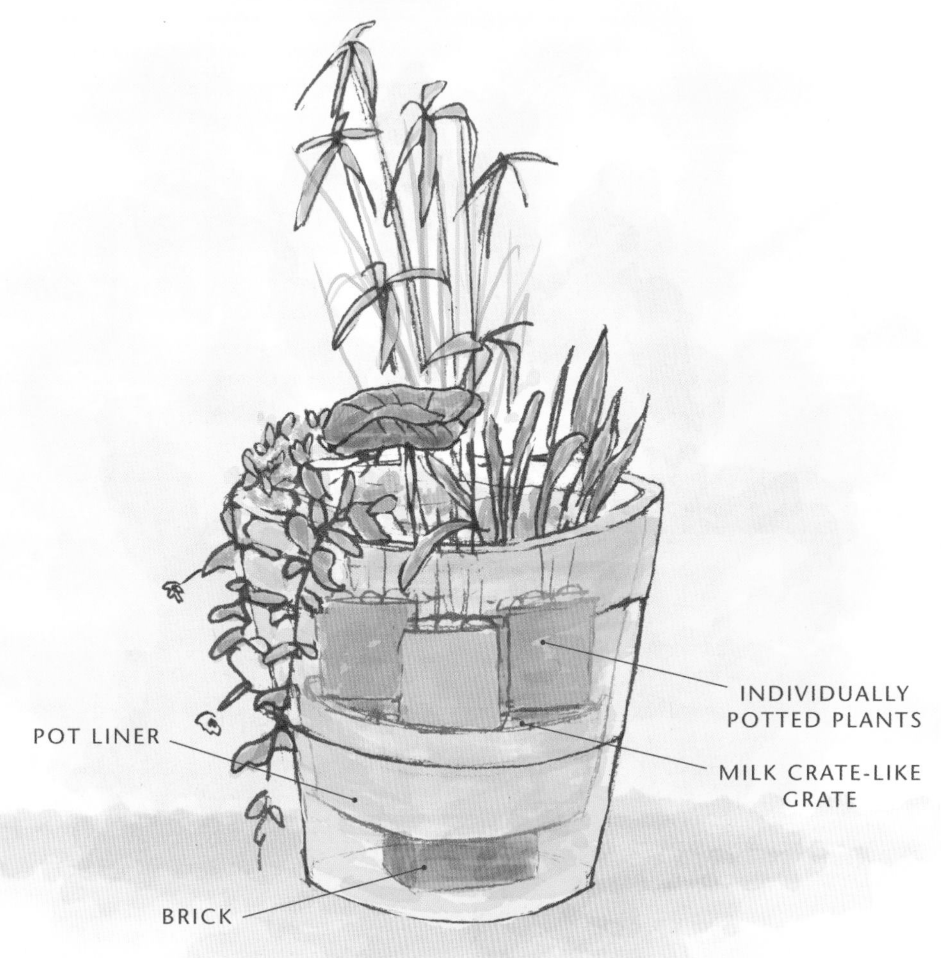

MATERIALS:

- **18-inch glazed ceramic pot**
- **Flexible, plastic pot liner**
- **Milk crate-like grate**
- **Bird feeder garden ornament**
- **Brick**
- **Assorted small river rocks**

PLANTS:

Water Zinnia (*Wedelia trilobata*)

Creeping Buttercup (*Ranunculus repens* 'Buttered Popcorn')

Blue Water Forget-Me-Not (*Myosotis scorpoides*)

Hardy Ground Orchid (*Bletillia striata*)

Narrow-leaved Arrowhead (*Sagittaria gramineus*)

Miniature Umbrella Palm (*Cyperus alternifolius* 'Gracilis')

TIPS:

Although this container had a drainage hole, the use of a pot liner meant plugging the hole was not necessary.

PROJECT SEVEN AQUA LIME

STEP 1:

Prepare the container.

Since we used a pot liner, there was no preparation necessary.

STEP 2:

Need a lift?

The liner was too short for the container, so a brick was placed at the bottom of the pot to raise it up a bit.

STEP 3:

Place the liner inside.

Place the liner in the pot so the top of the liner is even or slightly under the lip of the pot.

STEP 4:

Another lift.

After cutting the milk crate-like grate to the correct size so it sits at the water depth required by the plants, it can be positioned inside the pot.

STEP 5:

The final touches.

Place the plants and arrange small rocks so the growing pots cannot be seen. Eventually, when the plants grow, you won't be able to see the plastic liner. Don't forget to remove the plant tags!

STEP 6:

Fill the container with water.

Once the plants are in place, fill the container with water, being careful not to get a lot of water in between the pot and the liner.

FINAL

PROJECT EIGHT

ULTIMATE URN

MATERIALS:

- **Glazed ceramic urn with a 20-inch opening and 48 inches tall**
- **1500 gph pump**
- **1-inch bulkhead fitting**
- **AquaBasin™**
- **10-watt waterfall lights**
- **Light transformer**
- **250 to 500 lbs. of 2 to 3-inch river rock**
- **AquaBasin™ Kit or the following fittings:**

1-inch union fitting

1-inch MPT x barb fittings (4)

1-inch 90° elbow barb x barb fitting

1-inch MPT x slip fitting

Length of 1-inch schedule 40 pvc pipe

6-foot length of 1-inch vinyl tube

Stainless steel hose clamps

TIPS:

The use of a ball valve on this project would allow the water flow to be adjusted if needed.

PROJECT EIGHT ULTIMATE URN

STEP 1:

Pick the location.

Because of the large size of the container, it was located next to a large gazebo so it didn't look out of scale.

STEP 2:

Outline the AquaBasin™.

An AquaBasin™ is a new item that acts as a water holding basin for use in a project like this. Outline the AquaBasin™ with spray paint.

Note: An alternative to using an AquaBasin™ would be to dig a hole (large enough to hold the water capacity of the container you use) that is lined with rubber liner and filled with rock.

STEP 3:

Dig the hole.

Following the spray-painted line, dig a hole that is 14 to 16 inches deep. Add sand to help make sure that the inside of the hole is level.

STEP 4:

Install the AquaBasin™.

Place the AquaBasin™ into the hole that you dug.

STEP 5:
Check the level.

Using a 4-foot level, make sure that the AquaBasin™ is sitting level in the hole. If it is not, pull out the AquaBasin™ and re-adjust the soil or sand inside the hole.

STEP 6:
Drill the hole.

The container you choose may or may not have a hole in it. This one was smaller than the bulkhead fitting, so drilling a larger hole was required. Using duct tape and a homemade template, the hole was made larger with a masonry bit.

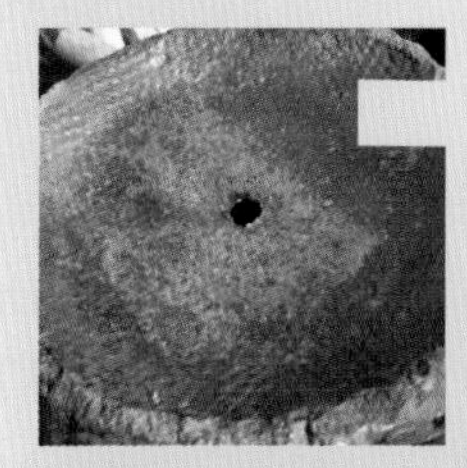

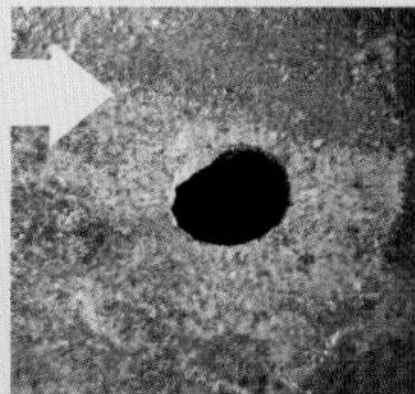

STEP 7:
Insert the bulkhead fitting.

The bulkhead fitting creates a seal around that hole where the pump and plumbing will enter the container.

STEP 8:
Connect the plumbing.

All the plumbing parts are connected to seamlessly join the container with the pump.

STEP 9:
Place the container.

Carefully place the container on top of the AquaBasin™.

ULTIMATE URN

STEP 10:

Check to make sure the urn is level.

The water will not flow equally out of the container if it is not level.

STEP 11:

Begin filling the basin with water.

While you finish up the last few steps, you can start filling the basin with water.

STEP 12:

Hook up the pump.

As the basin fills with water, place the pump into the AquaBasin™ and connect it to the bulkhead fitting.

STEP 13:

Hook up the stand pipe.

Insert the pvc pipe to the bulkhead fitting at the bottom of the urn. This pipe will help the water reach and overflow out of the top of the container without losing any force. This helps create a little bit of turbulence at the top of the urn.

STEP 14:

Add rocks.

Begin covering the top of the basin with rocks.

STEP 15:

Install the lighting.

Following manufacturers instructions, install the waterfall lights and the light transformer. Here, three lights were tucked into the rock at the base of the urn, equal distance apart. A fourth light was attached to the stand pipe to give the water a glow at night.

STEP 16:

Finish spreading the rocks.

Spread out the rest of the rocks, making sure the edges of the AquaBasin™ are covered.

STEP 17:

More water.

After the basin has been filled, don't forget to also fill the urn. Then, as the last step, rinse the dust off the rocks. The water will appear dirty at first but the dust will settle at the bottom of the basin and you'll enjoy crystal clear water.

Chapter 4

PLANTING & DESIGN

IDEAS FOR YOUR CONTAINER WATER GARDEN

Plants, of course, are what make your container water garden a garden. They add interest, texture, and a splash of color to the spot you choose for your garden. They also help keep the water clear of algae, while providing perching spots for birds that seek out the water. And if you're a gardener, what better way is there to explore a whole new exciting group of plants, than with aquatics?

NO LIMIT

There are a myriad of plants and flowers available for container water gardening, so there are few limits to the choices available in this rapidly-growing garden hobby. Not to mention the fact that your miniature water garden will provide something more unique than the standard geranium container with the ever-popular spike sprouting from the middle of the pot.

Aquatic plant types most commonly used in container water gardens include water lilies, marginals, and floaters. Water lilies really only work in very large containers because their leaves take up so much room. However, there are some varieties that are small enough to be used in smaller containers.

Most marginals are suited for growing in a container water garden. They come in all shapes and sizes from very slender and tall, to diminutive creepers that hang over the edge of the container. Some flower, while most are chosen for their foliage color or texture.

Since the plants will be in a contained growing environment, you don't need to be concerned with the spreading growth as much as you do the potential height of a plant. It is important to be aware of the potential height of the marginal plant that you choose so you don't plant one that grows to 6-plus feet in your table-top container water garden!

GARDEN TIP:

Traditional container gardens require frequent watering during the heat of the summer. If you prefer low-maintenance gardening, you'll appreciate the fact that the aquatic plants in your container water garden require much less water than traditional container plants.

GARDEN TIP:

Container water gardens are perfect vehicles for adding creativity and a wider variety of plants to your landscape. Open your yard and imagination to the possibilities provided by sprinkling your garden with these self-contained water gardens.

Water lilies really only work in very large containers because their leaves take up so much room. However, there are some varieties that are small enough to be used in smaller containers.

Take advantage of the extra space a large container provides, by including a water lily in your design.

A retail garden center may have a more limited plant selection than mail order, but you can buy larger, well-established plants.

Floaters are the workers of the container water garden plants. They fill in gaps left by young plants when a container is first planted and they absorb a great deal of the nutrients that cause algae growth. Because, they float, they're flexible too. Move them to a new spot or to a whole new container. They multiply fast, too! Starting with just one plant at the beginning of the season, you'll end up with enough "babies" to create a floater-only container water garden for yourself or as a gift.

Aquatic plants are available as hardy and tropical. Tropical plants are not hardy in in most areas of North America, but these are the most fun, provide the most thrill, the biggest bang with the loudest color, and the fastest growth. So even if you live up North, utilize plants that you like, not just plants that might handle the winter.

While the retail garden center offers larger, already potted and growing plants, the selection is usually limited to the most popular varieties.

CHOOSING YOUR PLANTS

Shopping for plants, whether by catalog or at a store, is an enjoyable activity for most gardeners. Traditionally, a catalog offers the widest selection of choices, but plants are usually shipped bare root and therefore need to be potted upon receipt and take time to reach an acceptable size. While the retail garden center offers larger, already potted and growing plants, the selection is usually limited to the most popular varieties.

You wouldn't plant sun-loving geraniums in a shady location, so ensure your aquatic gardening success by checking plant tags for exposure, plant growth, and flowering specifications.

Whichever route you choose for obtaining your plants, if you start with healthy, well-cared for plants, you will be successful in your new container water gardening hobby. When choosing the plants that will go into your container water garden, there are a few things you should consider first.

Location – Is the spot you chose sunny or shady? This information will, of course, determine the plants that you choose.

Color – What colors are in a nearby building, the flowers, or the patio accessories and furniture? Keep this in mind when choosing the colors of any blooming aquatic plants. So plants do not get lost, choose colors that do not match whatever is in the background of the container. With any other nearby colors, you could choose plants that match, complement, or contrast them. That's totally up to you and your personal taste and style.

Container – The size of the container will determine the size and quantity of plants that you'll need.

Assortment – For a container water garden arrangement that looks beautiful all season long, choose a wide assortment of plant types, shapes, and textures. Each container water garden should have at least one of the following plants:

Thriller – Plants that create drama from a distance. These are the focal point and draw attention to the container arrangement.

Filler – This plant gives the arrangement "body" and fills the center with plants that either compliment or contrast the thriller.

Spiller – Plants that break up and soften the edge of the pot by cascading over the edge. Not using a spiller causes a clear separation between bowl and plants.

DESIGNING YOUR CONTAINER

Simple and elegant. Overflowing and boisterous. The plants that you choose, along with the container they're planted in, create the personality and style of your container water garden. It's up to you which style you want to create.

A modest, elegant design is sleek and simple and might feature a tall, slender cattail surrounded by yellow creeping jenny that

THRILLERS, FILLERS, AND SPILLERS, OH MY!

Choose an assortment of plant types, shapes, and textures for a beautiful arrangement throughout the growing season. Each container water garden should have at least one of the following types of plants:

THRILLER

Plants that create drama from a distance. These are the focal point and draw attention to the container arrangement.

FILLER

This plant gives the arrangement "body" and fills the center with plants that either compliment or contrast the thriller.

SPILLER

Plants that break up and soften the edge of the pot by cascading over the edge. Not using a spiller causes a clear separation between bowl and plants.

STAR GRASS:

Similar to the famous poinsettia you buy for Christmas, this flower's petals are just colored leaves, leaving the impression it's in bloom all summer. It's not hardy, but it makes a great water plant for it perceived bright white flowers.

This overflowing and boisterous design features full plants that spill over the edge of the container.

over the edge of the container. Or it could be an upright horsetail and water lettuce floating on the water's surface.

An overflowing and boisterous design – like the person who's always the life of the party – is fun and full of life. This design might consist of a wild looking corkscrew rush, accented by a marsh marigold, with a splash of summer color coming from a spiky cardinal flower. The options are only limited by your imagination.

This modest and elegantly designed container features a tall thriller and a shorter filler, leaving room for a spiller and a water lily.

THE BASICS

Whatever type of design you decide to create, there are some basic design principals to keep in mind when planting your container water garden. In a traditional mixed container, it's usually best to place the tallest plant at the back of the container so you don't block the view of the shorter plants. Working your way toward the front of the container, place other upright plants that are a little shorter. Fill in with the rounded, or low growing filler plants. And finally, place the spiller plants at the front where they can spill over the front edge of the container. The spiller plants act as a connection of sorts between the plants and the container and help soften the hard line of the container's edge.

If your container water garden will be seen from all sides, plant it so the view will be pleasing all the way around. To do this, place the taller plants in the middle of the container and, working your way out to the edge of the pot, add the shorter plants around the perimeter. This method may require more plants than if you are creating a one-sided arrangement.

The plants that you choose, along with the container they're planted in, create the personality and style of your container water garden. It's up to you which style you want to create.

The arrangement of the plants depends on the shape of the container. Generally, it's best to plant in an asymmetrical pattern rather than straight rows, using an odd number of plants.

Most traditional container water gardens consist of an assortment of plants that are different heights, colors, and textures but it's not necessarily the only way it can be done. Beautiful and simple arrangements can be made up with only one or two plant types.

PLANTING YOUR CONTAINER

There are a number of ways you can go about planting your container water garden. Do you want an open pool of water, or do you like the look of exposed rock in your container? This is usually the determining factor when deciding how your container will be planted.

> **GARDEN TIP:**
>
> Fill your container with water the day before you plant it. This will allow the water to warm so it doesn't shock the new plants.

For an open pool of water (see Canteloupe Cabana on page 46), the plants are left in the growing containers and placed directly in the decorative pot that you chose. If your plant came in a small container, you should consider "bumping them up" or re-planting them into larger plastic pots for greater stability and more room for roots to grow. The growing pots can be disguised by the addition of some moss, rocks, or spiller plants. When planting in this way, you'll most likely need to find a way to raise the planting level up to where the plant's roots will be submerged under the appropriate water depth.

Another possibility is to fill the container with gravel and plant the aquatics directly into the rock (see Blue Moon on page 50). Leave an inch or so of space above the rock so there is room for some standing water. This is a container water garden, after all! With this planting method, it is best to take the plants out of the growing container and wash the soil from the roots.

To minimize the amount of rock needed, place an upside down pot at the bottom of the decorative container, then fill the remaining space with rock. In place of the upside down pot, you can also use large rocks or bricks – anything that will take up space to save on the amount of gravel you'll need.

A MATTER OF STYLE

You've planted your container water garden and are now feeling a sense of accomplishment, but as you step back to take a better look, you feel like something is missing. There are many decorative elements that you should consider to add a touch of style or whimsy to your project. Fountains, bubblers, statuary, or glass balls are among the possibilities, but before adding the fun, decorative touches, keep

your garden's style in mind. Formal, country, naturalistic, Mediterranean, or Asian. Whatever description best fits your garden style, you can find a container water garden style that complements it.

Landscaping in and around the yard primarily involves consideration of plant choices, but with a container water garden, the container itself adds a nice pop of color. This is important to the gardener who is limited in plant selection due to sun exposure, soil type, and soil drainage.

For example, shady areas don't provide the living conditions optimal for some of the vibrant, tropical colors found in sunny gardens. You can solve this color limitation problem by adding a brightly colored container or two to a shady corner of the yard, patio, or balcony and then mix it up with an interesting plant selection. Have fun planting!

CONTAINER WATER GARDEN PLANT GALLERY

Arrowhead
Sagittaria latifolia

ZONE 3 – 11
HEIGHT 24"

Arrow-shaped leaves on massive stems. This makes a great thriller for the container water garden.

Arrowhead, Narrow-leaved
Sagittaria gramineus

ZONE 3 – 9
HEIGHT 12"

Oblong, narrow leaves and tiny white flowers add a delicate touch to the container garden.

Bacopa, Lemon
Bacopa caroliniana

ZONE 7 – 11
HEIGHT 2 – 4"

A great spiller that cascades down the edge of the container. Also works well at the base of taller plants.

Calla Lily
Zantedeschia aethiopica

ZONE 6 – 11
HEIGHT 18"

Tropical looking foliage with a seductive flower.

Canna, Variegated
Canna 'Pretoria'

ZONE 7 – 10
HEIGHT 3 – 4'

Bright orange against purple, variegated leaves make this plant a definite thriller!

Cardinal Flower
Lobelia cardinalis

ZONE 5 – 9
HEIGHT 2 – 3'

Red flowers of this tall growing plants provide a splash of vibrant color to most green aquatics.

Photo by Florida Aquatic Nursery

Cattail, Miniature
Typha minima

ZONE 3 – 12
HEIGHT 12 – 18"

This miniature version of the well-known cattail has tiny, 1-inch, soft catkins on thin, strappy leaves.

Cattail, Variegated
Typha latifolia 'Variegata'

ZONE 4 – 11
HEIGHT 5 – 6'

This thriller of a plant adds brightness to the container water garden. The vertical variegated leaves are white with light green stripes, offering great companionship to others colors.

Creeping Buttercup
Ranunculus repens 'Buttered Popcorn'

ZONE 4 – 9
HEIGHT 8 – 10"

Beautiful green variegated, ruffled foliage and cute, little yellow buttercup flowers make this plant a winner for any container.

Creeping Jenny
Lysimachia nummularia

ZONE 4 – 10
HEIGHT 1 – 3"

The chartreuse, penny-sized leaves of this spiller grow almost anywhere, especially over the edges of the pot. A magnificent plant.

Fiber Optic Grass
Scirpus cernuus

ZONE 5
HEIGHT 10"

A big tuft of grassy foliage topped with tiny brown flowers make the name of this filler obvious!

Forget-Me-Not
Myosotis scorpoides

ZONE 3 – 9
HEIGHT 2 – 6"

Tiny blue flowers with a dot of yellow in the center make this spiller a favorite container water garden addition.

GROWER PICK = *Container Water Garden Favorites*

PLANT GALLERY CONTAINER WATER GARDEN

Horsetail, Dwarf
Equisetum scirpoides

ZONE 4 – 9
HEIGHT 8″

With classic, horsetail-jointed stems, this mini version works well in small containers where the larger version won't.

Horsetail
Equisetum hyemale

ZONE 4 – 11
HEIGHT 24″

Straight from the dinosaur age, horsetail, with it's interesting, jointed stems, does great in a sunny container water garden.

Iris, Japanese
Iris ensata 'Variegata'

ZONE 5 – 10
HEIGHT 3 – 4′

Sword shaped leaves show off nice, green and white vertical stripes. The flowers are spectacular, but the foliage is what counts most.

Marble Queen
Echinodorus cordifolius 'Marble Queen'

ZONE 7 – 10
HEIGHT 24″

A terrific plant with cool, variegated leaves and runners that cascade over the edges in an attempt to grow little baby plants along the stem.

Marestail
Hippurus vulgaris

ZONE 4
HEIGHT 8 – 12″

Similar to parrots feather, this feathery foliage adds a soft touch as it fills in the bare spots of your container garden.

Marsh Marigold
Caltha palustris

ZONE 3 – 9
HEIGHT 12″

An outstanding filler plant with early yellow blooms that return to greet you every spring.

Papyrus, Dwarf
Cyperus isocladus

ZONE 8 – 10
HEIGHT 24 – 30″

Add a splash of the tropics with this thriller of a plant!

Papyrus, Giant Dwarf
Cyperus percamenthus

ZONE 9 – 10
HEIGHT 12 – 28″

Giant, fluffy papyrus heads adorn the tops of stout stems.

Parrots Feather
Myriophyllum aquatica

ZONE 6 – 10
HEIGHT 6″

Feathery, gray foliage creates a soft mat that spills over the edge of the container.

Parrots Feather, Red-stemmed
Myriophyllum brasiliense

ZONE 5
HEIGHT 8 – 12″

The same feathery foliage and great habit as M. aquatica, but with vibrant red stems.

Pennywort, Variegated
Hydrocotyle sibthorpioides 'Variegata'

ZONE 6 – 10
HEIGHT 1″

Tiny scalloped and light green leaves look as though they've been dipped in white chocolate.

Pickerel Plant
Pontederia cordata

ZONE 3 – 8
HEIGHT 24 – 30″

This filler features lush foliage and bright blue flowers that bloom a long time.

GROWER PICK = *Container Water Garden Favorites*

CONTAINER WATER GARDEN PLANT GALLERY

Rush, Common
Juncus effuses

ZONE 3 – 9
HEIGHT 2′

Tubular leaves spike upward toward the sky.

Rush, Spiral
Juncus effuses 'Spiralis'

ZONE 5 – 8
HEIGHT 12 – 18″

A spiller and a thriller with unique, spiraled stems shoot upwards from the center of the plant. An eye catcher to anyone.

Society Garlic
Tulbaghia violacea 'Variegata'

ZONE 5 – 9
HEIGHT 12 – 24″

White and green variegated foliage shoot spikes of pink flowers like fireworks all summer.

Spearwort, Small Creeping
Ranumculus flammula

ZONE 3 – 9
HEIGHT 6 – 8″

Small green leaves are hardly noticed behind the veil of tiny yellow flowers that spill out of the container.

Star Grass
Dichromena colorata

ZONE 8 – 10
HEIGHT 12 – 24″

This plant appears to be flowering all the time with little stars of blooms that float above the plant.

Sweetflag, Dwarf Variegated
Acorus gramineus 'Ogon'

ZONE 5 – 9
HEIGHT 12″

This flexible plant is ideal for container water gardens as it tolerates a range of water depths. A real beauty.

Taro, Black Magic
Colocasia esculenta 'Black Magic'

ZONE 8 – 10
HEIGHT 4 – 5′

Large, elephant ear-shaped leaves on large clumps offer a thriller of a dramatic backdrop to place other contrasting plants against.

Taro, Imperial
Colocasia esculenta 'Imperial'

ZONE 8 – 10
HEIGHT 4 – 5′

Green arrowhead-shaped leaves have a splash of purple in the center.

Taro, Red Stemmed
Colocasia 'Fontenessii'

ZONE 8 – 10
HEIGHT 36″

Glossy green leaves on deep purple stems. Grows a little taller than 'Black Magic' and forms less of a clump. Each leaf is a work of art.

Thalia, Powdery
Thalia dealabata

ZONE 8 – 10
HEIGHT 6′

Gray foliage of the thalia is what counts the most, and the odd angle of the leaves alone are a statement of character and personality.

Thalia, Red-Stemmed
Thalia geniculata f. rumnoides

ZONE 5
HEIGHT 2 – 10′

This plant shows off well by itself, or in combo with others. The bright red stems with contrasting green leaves are awesome.

Umbrella Palm, Miniature
Cyperus alternifolius 'Gracilis'

ZONE 9 – 11
HEIGHT 24″

Bursts of green leaves atop 2-foot stems create little umbrellas of green in your container water garden.

Photo by Florida Aquatic Nursery

GROWER PICK = *Container Water Garden Favorites*

PLANT GALLERY CONTAINER WATER GARDEN

Water Clover, Upright
Marsilea quadrifolia

ZONE 6
HEIGHT 2 – 6″

The softest of green four leaf clovers spreads and spills throughout your container water garden.

Water Hyacinth
Eichhornia crassipes

ZONE 9 – 11
HEIGHT 6″

Indispensable to any water feature, this plant cleans the water while rewarding you with pretty lavender flowers.

Water Lettuce
Pistia stratiotes

ZONE 9 – 11
HEIGHT 8″

Soft and velvety, this floating plant can adorn any space in a container water garden.

Yerba Mansa
Anemopsis californica

ZONE 4 – 10
HEIGHT 6″

White petals surround a white, cone-shaped center. As they age, the flowers get pink spots. Blooms all summer.

HARDY WATER LILIES FOR CONTAINER WATER GARDENS

Photo by Florida Aquatic Nursery

Chrysantha

FLOWER SIZE: 3 – 4″ SPREAD: 2 – 3′
FLOWER COLOR: YELLOW/ORANGE

Comanche

FLOWER SIZE: 3 – 5″ SPREAD: 3 – 5′
FLOWER COLOR: CHANGEABLE YELLOW TO ORANGE

Photo by Florida Aquatic Nursery

Helvola

FLOWER SIZE: 2 – 3″ SPREAD: 2 – 3′
FLOWER COLOR: LIGHT YELLOW

Hermine

FLOWER SIZE: 4 – 5″ SPREAD: 2 – 3′
FLOWER COLOR: WHITE

TROPICAL WATER LILIES FOR CONTAINER WATER GARDENS

Dauben

FLOWER SIZE: 4 – 6″ SPREAD: 3 – 7′
FLOWER COLOR: LIGHT BLUE

Red Flare

FLOWER SIZE: 6 – 10″ SPREAD: 6′
FLOWER COLOR: MAROON

Photo by Florida Aquatic Nursery

Star of Siam

FLOWER SIZE: 4 – 6″ SPREAD: 6′
FLOWER COLOR: BLUE

Panama Pacific

FLOWER SIZE: 5 – 7″ SPREAD: 4 – 6′
FLOWER COLOR: PLUM

GROWER PICK = *Container Water Garden Favorites*

DESIGN IDEA #1 ROYAL FAMILY

A

B

C

D

ROYAL FAMILY — DESIGN IDEA #1

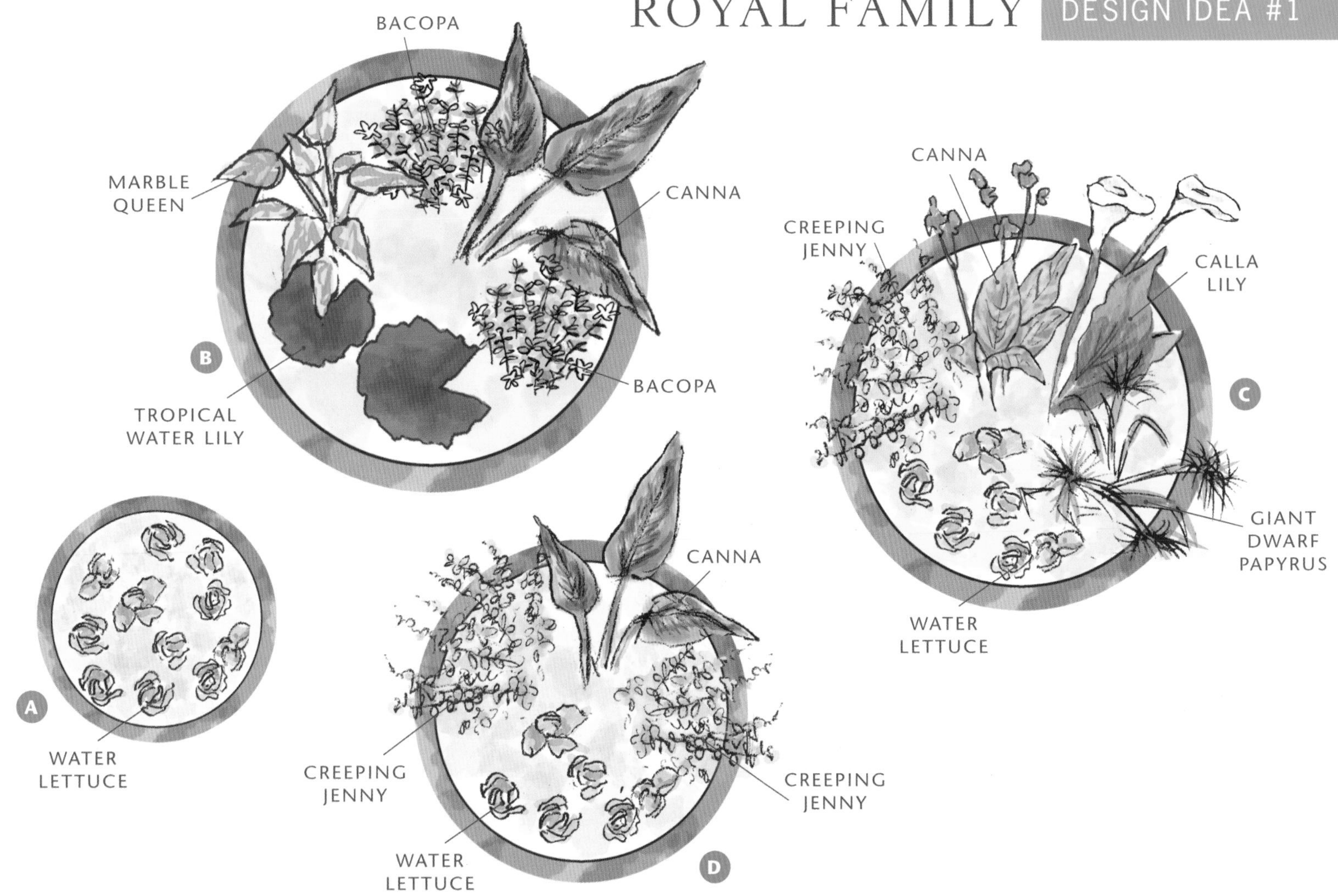

BACOPA
MARBLE QUEEN
CANNA
BACOPA
TROPICAL WATER LILY
B
CANNA
CREEPING JENNY
CALLA LILY
C
GIANT DWARF PAPYRUS
WATER LETTUCE
A
WATER LETTUCE
CANNA
CREEPING JENNY
CREEPING JENNY
WATER LETTUCE
D

MATERIALS:

- **Low-profile, ceramic water garden pots**
- **Bricks or rock to raise the planting level to the appropriate depth for the plants you've chosen**

PLANTS: (POT A)

Water Lettuce *(Pistia stratiotes)*

PLANTS: (POT B)

Bronze Canna *(Canna australis)*

Lemon Bacopa *(Bacopa caroliniana)*

Tropical Water Lily 'Red Flare'

Marble Queen *(Echinodorus cordifolius* 'Marble Queen')

PLANTS: (POT C)

Giant Dwarf Papyrus *(Cyperus percamenthus)*

Water Lettuce *(Pistia stratiotes)*

Yellow Creeping Jenny *(Lysimachia nummularia* 'Aurea')

Calla Lily *(Zantedeschia aethiopica)*

PLANTS: (POT D)

African Sunset Canna (*Canna* 'African Sunset')

Yellow Creeping Jenny (*Lysimachia nummularia* 'Aurea')

Water Lettuce *(Pistia stratiotes)*

TIPS:

- A grouping of containers in a strong color like this bright, cobalt blue makes a strong statement on an intimate patio.
- A red-leaved water lily provides a nice contrast or complement, depending on the color of container you choose.
- A plant that spills over the edge, like the marble queen in pot B, helps soften the hard line of the pot's edge.

DESIGN IDEA #2 AMERI-COOL

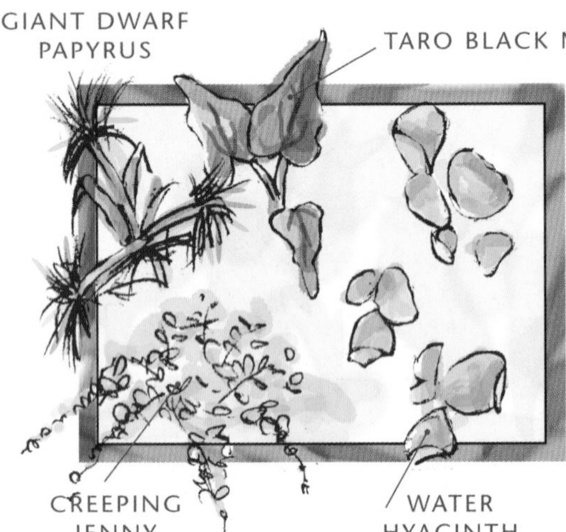

MATERIALS:

- **Any interesting found container**
- **Bricks or rock to raise the planting level to the appropriate depth for the plants you've chosen**
- **Get some twine to tie an old bottle opener to the side to complete the look**

PLANTS:

Water Hyacinth *(Eichhornia crassipes)*

Black Magic Taro *(Colocasia* 'Black Magic'*)*

Yellow Creeping Jenny *(Lysimachia nummularia* 'Aurea'*)*

Giant Dwarf Papyrus *(Cyperus percamenthus)*

TIPS:

- A found object like this antique Coca-Cola cooler adds a touch of Americana to your outdoor space.
- The ball-shaped spheres of Giant Dwarf Papyrus are a great contrast to the delicate foliage of the 'Black Magic' taro.
- Over time, taro can grow into a large plant with lots of side shoots and multiple stems. Consider over-wintering this plant indoors if you live in a cold climate.
- Sunny or shady – taro does well in high and low light situations, but the more sun 'Black Magic' gets, the blacker it's foliage becomes.
- Don't add ice cubes!!

EARTHTONE TRIO DESIGN IDEA #3

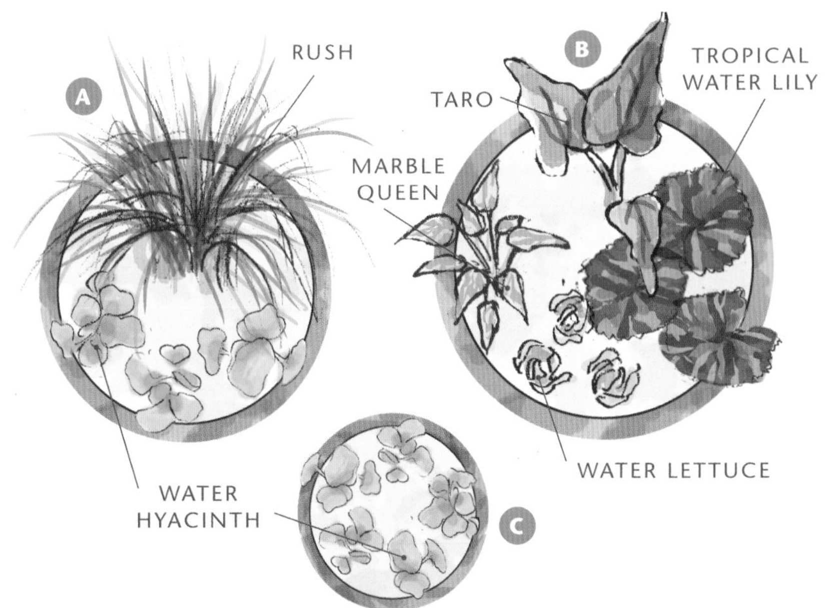

TIPS:

- Water hyacinth works hard in any container water garden to help keep the water clean and also acts as a nice filler.
- 'Carmen's Grey' rush provides an explosion of grey needles.
- To raise plants up to the proper planting depth, 8-inch square pots and 17-inch kidney shaped baskets can be used with special basket hooks.
- The warm water of a container water garden helps tropical water lilies bloom earlier than when they are in a larger volume of water, like a pond, which stays cooler.
- Grouping several containers together has a nice impact on a large patio.

MATERIALS:

- **Assorted containers**
- **Plant baskets**
- **Basket hooks**
- **Aquatic potting soil**

PLANTS: (POT A)

Carmen's Grey Rush
(*Juncus patens* 'Carmen's Grey')

Water Hyacinth
(Eichhornia crassipes)

PLANTS: (POT B)

Red-Stemmed Taro
(*Colocasia* 'Fontenessii')

Tropical Water Lily
'Star of Siam'

Marble Queen *(Echinodorus cordifolius* 'Variegata')

PLANTS: (POT C)

Water Hyacinth
(Eichhornia crassipes)

DESIGN IDEA #4

CREEPING CAULDRON

MATERIALS:

- **A container that can be tilted at an interesting angle**

PLANTS:

Water Hyacinth *(Eichhornia crassipes)*

Yellow Creeping Jenny *(Lysimachia nummularia* 'Aurea'*)*

TIPS:

- Simplicity is a form of art.
- Water hyacinth maintains the water quality and helps keep it free from algae.
- Creeping Jenny flows gracefully out of the front of this tilted container to create the effect of spilling water.

RUSTIC ROOTS

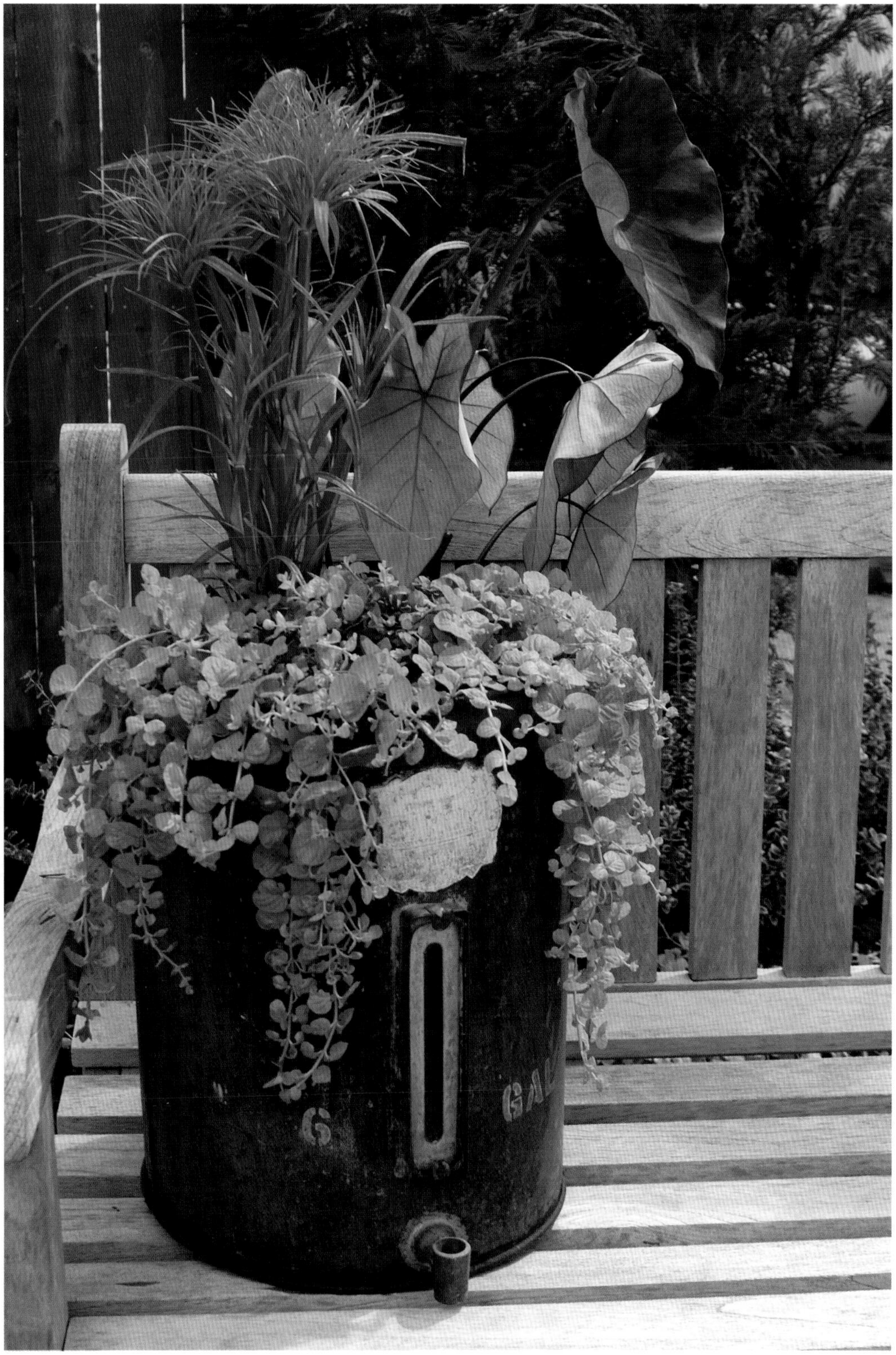

MATERIALS:

- **Interesting, found container**
- **Pea gravel**

PLANTS:

Giant Dwarf Papyrus
(Cyperus percamenthus)

Red-Stemmed Taro
***(Colocasia* 'Fontenessii')**

Yellow Creeping Jenny
***(Lysimachia nummularia* 'Aurea')**

TIPS:

- Any interesting found object that holds water – like this cream separator – makes a great addition your outdoor living area, as well as a conversation piece.
- Fill half way with gravel and set the potted plants on top. Fill the rest of the way with water.
- So easy to maintain but looks amazing, don't you agree?

DESIGN IDEA #6 KETTLE KABOODLE

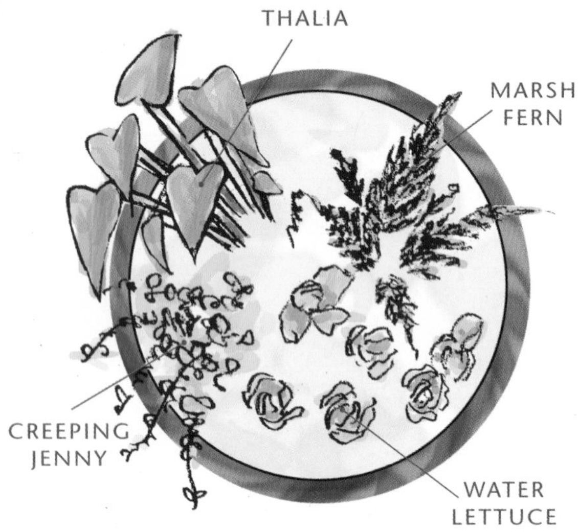

MATERIALS:

- Bricks to build the plants up to the correct planting level
- Small stones to weight down the plants or larger aquatic plant pots for re-potting

PLANTS:

Red-Stemmed Thalia ***(Thalia geniculata*** **'Rumnoides')**

Yellow Creeping Jenny ***(Lysimachia nummularia*** **'Aurea')**

Water Lettuce ***(Pistia stratiotes)***

Marsh Fern ***(Thelepteris palustris)***

TIPS:

- Use colorful foliage to steal the show in your container water garden. The bright red stems of red-stemmed thalia become more pronounced as they mature.
- Experiment with unexpected plants like the marsh fern – one of the few ferns that can handle standing water. It is used very successfully to add more green shape to the simple aqua bowl.

DOUBLE TUBBOWL

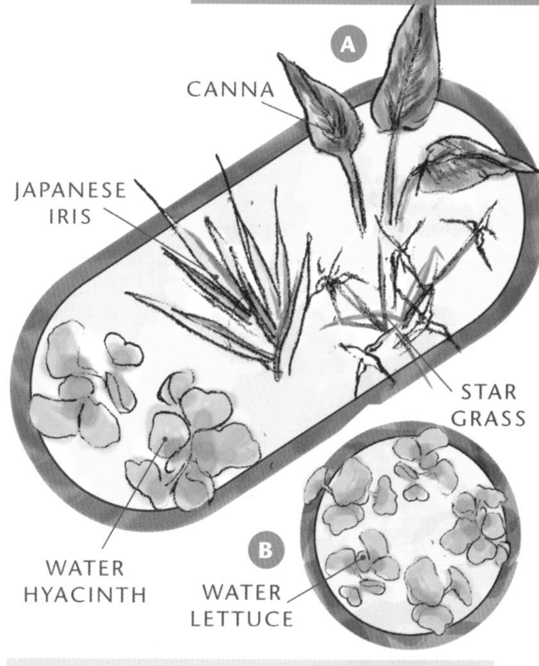

MATERIALS:

- **Bricks to build the plants up to the correct planting level**
- **Small stones to weight down the plants or larger aquatic plant pots for re-potting**

PLANTS: (POT A)

Water Hyacinth *(Eichhornia crassipes)*

Japanese Iris *(Iris ensata* 'Variegata' aka *Iris kaempherii* 'Variegata')

Star Grass *(Dichromena colorata)*

African Sunset Canna *(Canna* 'African Sunset')

PLANTS: (POT B)

Water Lettuce *(Pistia stratiotes)*

TIPS:

- Give an old item a new use like this oval copper kettle that was once used as a boiler to make fruit jams. Wood was put at the bottom to make sure the water would circulate under the jars.
- Choose striking variegated foliage. The variegated leaves of Japanese iris – one of the most useful irises – add color and light to the container, even when it's not in bloom.
- Not every container water garden needs a lot of plants. Often a simple version adds lots of interest to the corner of the patio. Add some floaters, some fish ... and the water remains clean and healthy.

DESIGN IDEA #8 BLACK MAGIC

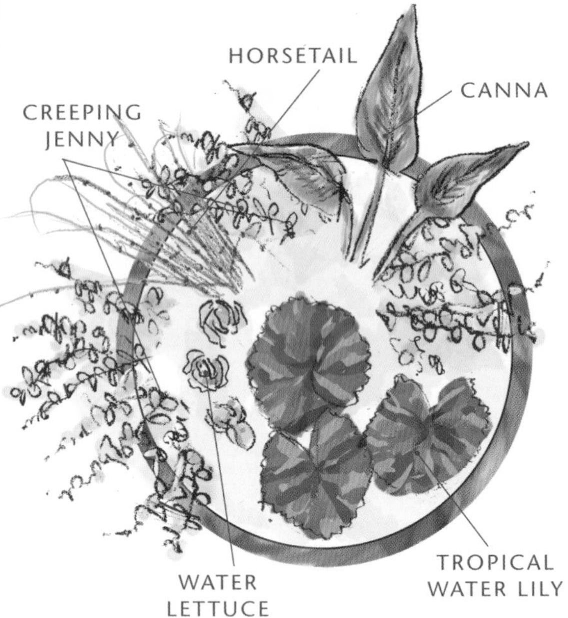

MATERIALS:

- **Bricks to build the plants up to the correct planting level**
- **Small stones to weight down the plants or larger aquatic plant pots for re-potting**

PLANTS:

Water Lettuce *(Pistia stratiotes)*

Yellow Creeping Jenny *(Lysimachia nummularia* 'Aurea')

Tropical Water Lily 'Queen of Siam' *(Nymphoides* 'Queen of Siam')

Horsetail *(Equisetum hyemale)*

Red-Leaved Canna *(Canna australis)*

TIPS:

- Use water lilies to really add a splash of color and class to your container water garden.
- Use contrasting colors like the chartreuse of yellow creeping Jenny near the purple of the canna.

RED ROVER DESIGN IDEA #9

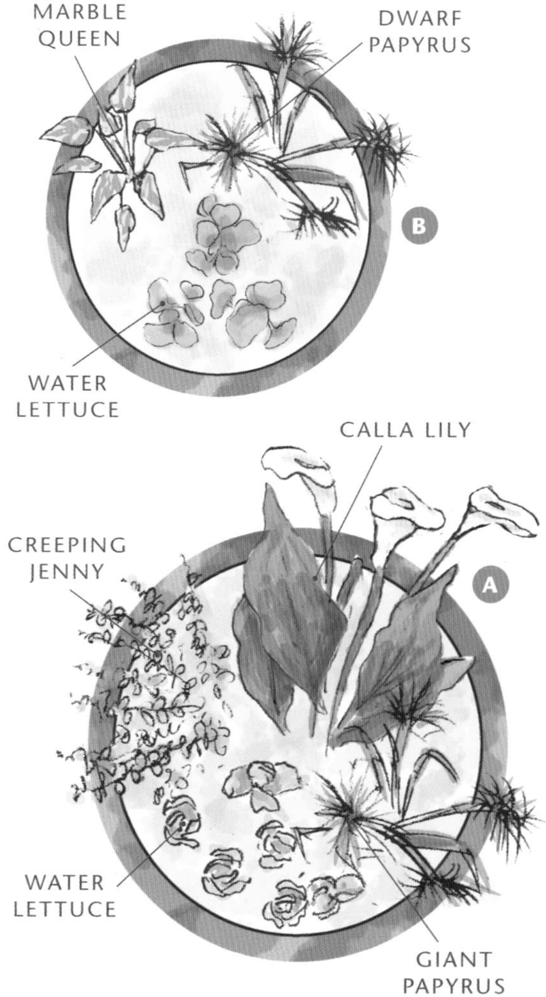

MATERIALS:

- **Two matching containers create a nice accent to the corner of a large patio, but it's not necessary**
- **Pick your favorite plant combination and just do one if you like**

PLANTS: (POT A)

Water Lettuce *(Pistia stratiotes)*

Yellow Creeping Jenny *(Lysimachia nummularia* 'Aurea'*)*

Giant Dwarf Papyrus *(Cyperus percamenthus)*

Calla Lily *(Zantdeschia aethiopica)*

PLANTS: (POT B)

Water Hyacinth *(Eichhornia crassipes)*

Dwarf Payprus *(Cyperus isocladus)*

Marble Queen *(Echinodorus cordifolius* 'Variegata'*)*

TIPS:

- A container water garden can be as simple or as complex as you like. Either of these would be great with the addition of a small pump to create some water movement and sound.
- Floating plants are versatile and can be placed anywhere in your container water garden. They're hard workers too – helping keep the water clean by absorbing a large amount of nutrients through their roots.

DESIGN IDEA #10 PAIL GREENS

MATERIALS:

- A few rocks to bring the planting up to the proper water depth
- You can either plant the aquatics right in the rocks or set the planting containers on top of the rocks

PLANTS:

Spiral Rush *(Juncus effuses* 'Spiralis')

Yellow Creeping Jenny *(Lysimachia nummularia* 'Aurea')

TIPS:

- Choose plants that will flow over the edge of the container. They soften the edges of the containers and bring the eye down instead of just up, following the larger upright plant.

Below: Simplicity is elegant; even when it's floating in an antique enamelware bowl. When using water hyacinth alone in a bowl, be sure to refresh the water regularly (once every 1-2 weeks). If plants become yellow, remove some and add some water soluble fertilizer to keep them lush and green.

Above: Cut leaves and flowers from most any aquatic plant and float them in your favorite water-filled bowl. Choose flower buds from one or more types of plants or colors of water lilies. This is a great way to add instant and interesting color to your outdoor entertaining area.

GAZING GARDEN GLORY

DESIGN IDEA #11

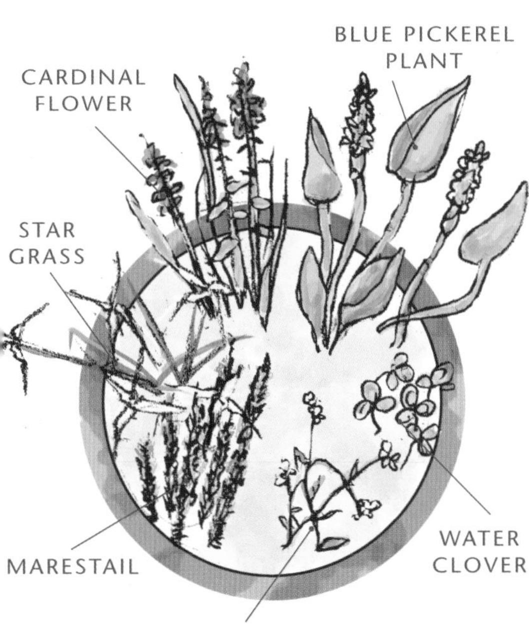

MATERIALS:

- 18-inch decorative pot
- Black plastic milk crate-like grate
- Cork
- Silicone sealant
- 2 to 3-inch river rock
- Colorful glass fishing floats

PLANTS:

Blue Pickerel Plant *(Pontederia cordata)*

Water Clover *(Marsilea mutica)*

Blue Water Forget-Me-Not *(Myosotis scirpoides)*

Marestail *(Hippurus vulgaris)*

Star Grass *(Dichromena colorata)*

Queen Victoria Cardinal Flower *(Lobelia cardinalis* 'Queen Victoria')

TIPS:

- Adding a container water garden to your perennial border adds a little hardscape accent and nicely compliments the adjacent flowers.
- If it can be located near an outlet, add a pump or fountain to bring the sound of water out into the landscape.
- A household cork can be used to plug small holes of some containers.
- Colorful glass fishing floats add a touch of interest and can be lit from underneath with a small, 10-watt waterfall light for a night time accent.

DESIGN IDEA #12 BENCH WARMER

MATERIALS:

- Bricks to build the plants up to the correct planting level
- Small stones to weight down the plants or larger aquatic plant pots for re-potting

PLANTS:

Water Hyacinth
(Eichhornia crassipes)

African Sunset Canna
(*Canna* 'African Sunset')

Black Gamecock Iris
(*Iris* 'Black Gamecock')

TIPS:

- Use any variety of canna or iris, depending on your choice of colors.
- A square container instead of the usual round one creates a more contemporary look on your patio.

HARVEST PUMPKIN

DESIGN IDEA #13

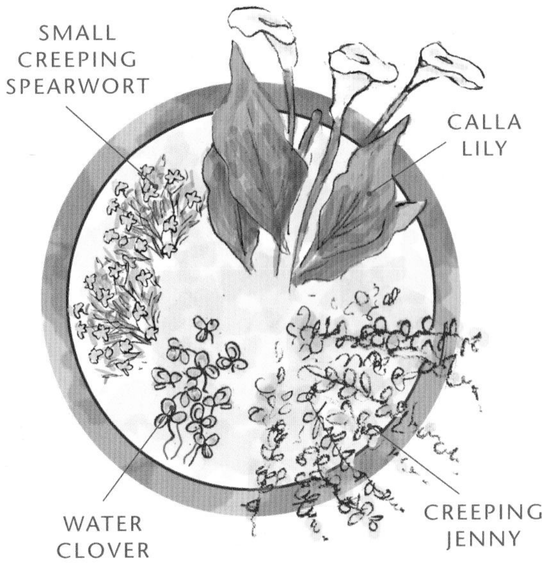

MATERIALS:

- **Spray-on water sealant**
- **2 to 3-inch river rock**
- **11-inch terra cotta pot**

PLANTS:

Calla Lily *(Zantedeschia aethiopica)*

Small Creeping Spearwort *(Ranunculus flammula)*

Water Clover *(Marsilea mutica)*

Yellow Creeping Jenny *(Lysimachia nummularia)*

TIPS:

- Plants were removed from their growing containers and planted directly into the rock.
- The water in your container will evaporate. Be sure to top it off as needed, based on evaporation rate.
- This easy planter makes a great outdoor centerpiece.

DESIGN IDEA #14 QUEEN'S DELIGHT

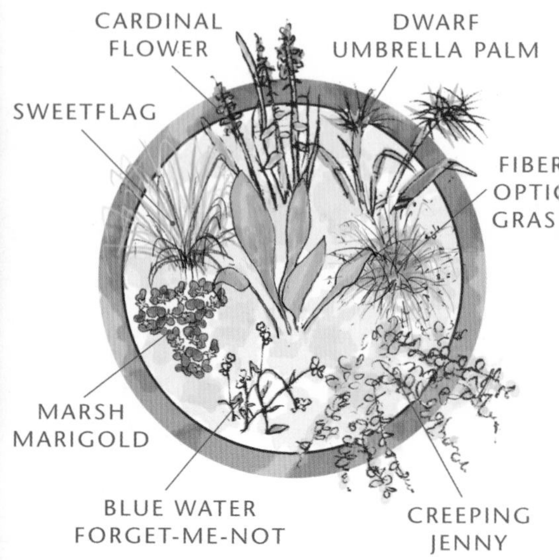

MATERIALS:

- 26-inch terra cotta pot
- Milk crate-like black plastic grate
- 2 to 3-inch river rock
- Large rubber plug
- Spray-on water sealant
- Copper dragonfly fountain with pump

PLANTS:

Queen Victoria Cardinal Flower ***(Lobelia cardinalis*** **'Queen Victoria')**

Dwarf Umbrella Palm ***(Cyperus alternifolius*** **'Gracillis')**

Fiber Optic Grass ***(Scirpus cernuus)***

Narrow-Leaved Arrowhead ***(Sagittaria gramineus)***

Yellow Creeping Jenny ***(Lysimachia nummularia)***

Blue Water Forget-Me-Not ***(Myosotis scirpoides)***

Marsh Marigold ***(Caltha palustris)***

Dwarf Variegated Sweetflag ***(Acorus gramineus*** **'Ogon')**

QUEEN'S DELIGHT DESIGN IDEA #14

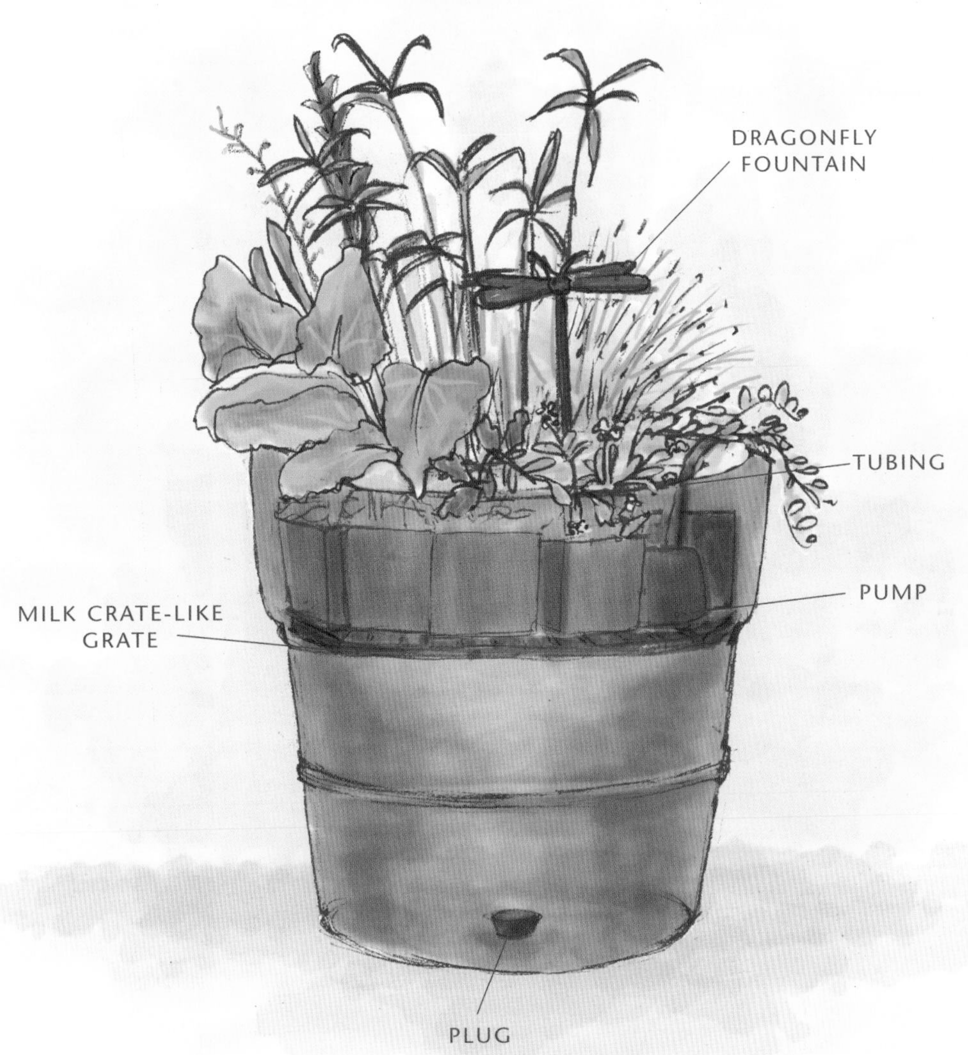

TIPS:

- The black plastic milk crate-like grate was cut to size so it would sit inside the pot about 4 to 6 inches from the top, providing a shelf at the appropriate water depth for the aquatic plants.
- Plants left in their small growing pots can sometimes float or be difficult to keep in place. Small river rocks set on top of the pot's soil surface weigh them down to keep them in place while helping to disguise the pots.
- This dragonfly fountain creates a peaceful dripping sound and adds a touch of whimsy to the container water garden.
- Leave a little bit of exposed water for the fountain to drip into for a more dramatic effect.

DESIGN IDEA #15

MORNING RAIN

MATERIALS:

- EPDM Rubber liner
- 20-inch terra cotta pot
- 18-inch plastic or terra cotta saucer
- 75 gph statuary pump
- Cinder block
- 2 to 3-inch river rock
- 6 to 8-inch boulders
- Moss or burlap
- ⅜-inch clear vinyl tubing

PLANTS:

Variegated Cattail
(Typha latifolia 'Variegata')

Dwarf Papyrus *(Cyperus haspen)*

Marestail *(Hippurus vulgaris)*

Creeping Buttercup
(Ranunculus 'Buttered Popcorn')

Lemon Bacopa *(Bacopa caroliniana)*

Dwarf Variegated Sweetflag
(Acorus gramineus 'Ogon')

Small Creeping Spearwort
(Ranunculus flammula)

MORNING RAIN

DESIGN IDEA #15

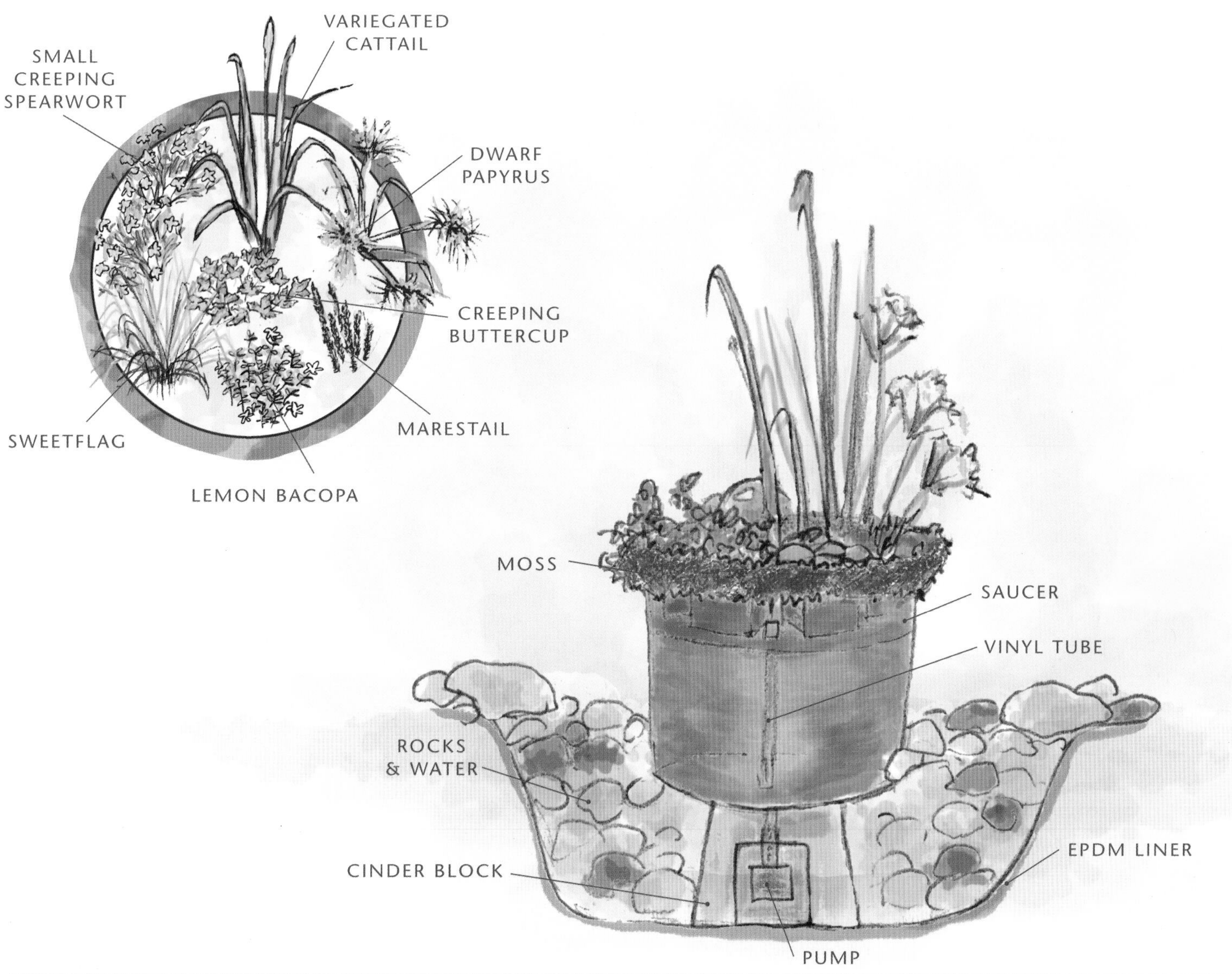

TIPS:

- The rock-filled hole is lined with EPDM rubber to hold the water that is re-circulated up into the pot and over the edge, dripping back into the rocks.
- The hole should be large enough to hold how ever many gallons of water your pot holds.
- The cinder block provides a steady surface to rest the pot and the small pump fits nicely into one of the holes.
- Cut a hole in the plastic saucer for the tube to supply moving water to the top of the pot, ready to trickle to the rocks below.
- Moss was originally used around this container to create the delicate dripping however, birds found this much too tempting to resist and stole it for their nests. The moss was replaced with a 4-inch wide strip of burlap that, when applied wet, easily stayed in place to create a nice drip pattern.
- Rocks around the perimeter help naturalize this feature.

DESIGN IDEA #16

MELLOW YELLOW

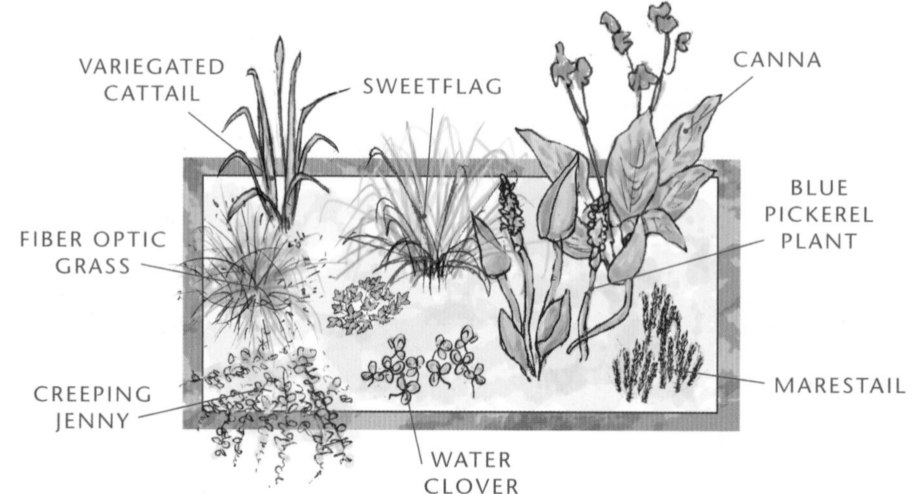

MATERIALS:

- **Old barn sink**
- **Assorted bricks**

PLANTS:

Variegated Canna (*Canna* 'Pretoria')

Blue Pickerel Plant (*Pontederia cordata*)

Marestail (*Hippurus vulgaris*)

Water Clover (*Marsilea mutica*)

Dwarf Variegated Sweetflag (*Acorus gramineus* 'Ogon')

Creeping Buttercup (*Ranunculus repens* 'Buttered Popcorn')

Yellow Creeping Jenny (*Lysimachia nummularia*)

Fiber Optic Grass (*Scirpus cernuus*)

Variegated Cattail (*Typha latifolia* 'Variegata')

TIPS:

- As simple as can be. Scout your favorite flea market for an old wash tub or barn sink, add some bricks if needed to get the plants up to proper water depth.
- The chartreuse shade of green in most of these plants makes a nice contrast to the green of the vegetable garden where this container sits.

POMP & CIRCUMSTANCE

DESIGN IDEA #17

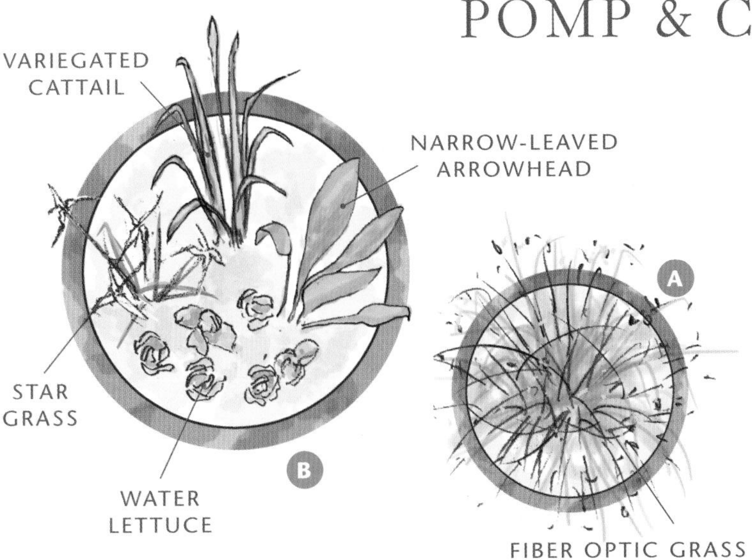

MATERIALS:

- **Ceramic pots – two sizes**
- **Black plastic milk crate-like grate**
- **2 to 3-inch river rock**

PLANTS:

Variegated Cattail *(Typha latifolia* 'Variegata')

Narrow-leaved Arrowhead *(Sagittaria gramineus)*

Star Grass *(Dichromena colorata)*

Fiber Optic Grass *(Scirpus cernuus)*

Water Lettuce *(Pistia stratiotes)*

TIPS:

- Buying pots without holes makes it even easier to get started on your project!
- A grouping of just two of the same pots makes this garden entrance a welcoming place to stop for a look.
- Red pots among all the green foliage add a pop of unexpected color.
- Look for a microbial larvicide designed to kill mosquito larvae for use in containers that do not having moving water.
- Your planting design can be as simple as a single fiber optic plant in a sleek, architectural pot.
- Use the river rock to hide pots and help keep them from floating out of place, or fill the container with them and plant the aquatics directly in the rock.

DESIGN IDEA #18 ZEN OASIS

MATERIALS:

- 75 gph statuary pump
- 6-inch square aquatic planting basket
- 1 to 2 inch river rock
- Cement leaves
- ¼-inch vinyl tubing
- Concrete trough

PLANTS:

Horsetail ***(Equisetum hyemale)***

Parrots Feather ***(Myriophyllum aquatica)***

ZEN OASIS DESIGN IDEA #18

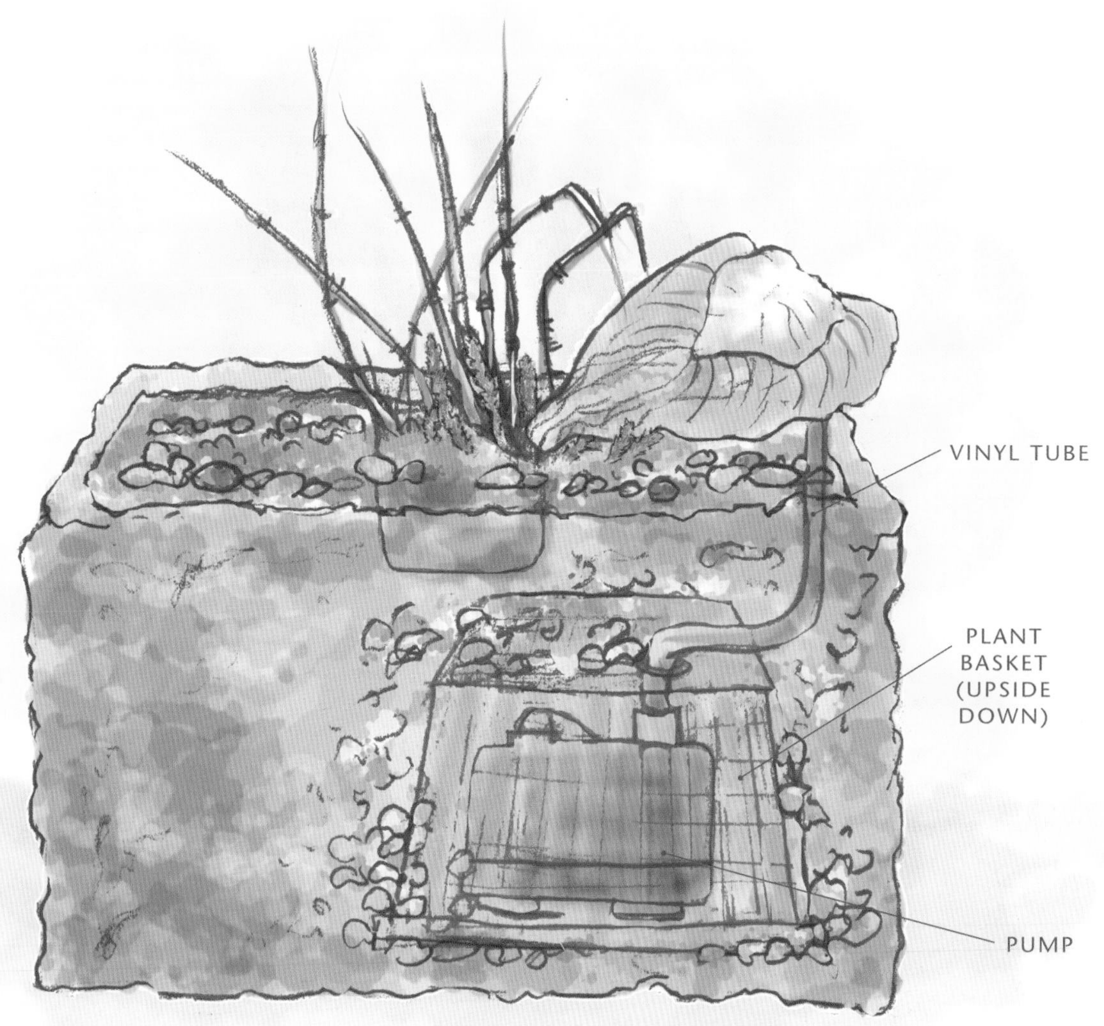

TIPS:

- Although most of this container is filled with river rock, putting a plant basket over the pump creates an area where no rock is needed, leaving more space for water. This keeps the pump operating which means it won't need to be re-filled as often.
- The basket also keeps rock from sitting directly around the pump.
- Cut a hole in the pot so the tube can pass through on it's way up to the fountain.
- Look for items like these hand made cement leaves to create interesting fountains.
- Making your own fountain means you have a one-of-a-kind water feature.
- Use flexible, vinyl tubing to connect the pump to your fountain. This can be purchased at most home stores or aquarium supply stores.
- Add as many or as few plants as you desire.
- If you fill the container all the way – so the rocks are under water – the rocks may turn green with algae. The addition of snails will consume some of the algae.
- For a different effect, fill the container to just below the level of the rocks. The top rocks will be dry, eliminating the cause of the algae.

Chapter 5

CARING FOR

YOUR CONTAINER WATER GARDEN

As you learned in previous chapters, container water gardens are like miniature ponds and can be a low maintenance, easy-to-grow, beautiful addition to your landscaping or outdoor living area. With a little care, they'll remain healthy all season long.

Like all good gardens, container water gardens require a little work in order to reap the fullest benefits from season to season. Sometimes, the work is little more than adding water to the container. Sometimes it may mean feeding your plants and thinning or removing excessive plant growth at the end of the growing season, cleaning algae off the sides of the container, or changing water occasionally. And for enthusiastic gardeners, it really doesn't feel like work at all!

ALGAE – IT'S NOT REALLY MUCH OF A FIGHT

If your container has standing or moving water, it has the potential to grow algae. The best way to control algae is to find something, or things, that will help consume the nutrients that the algae feeds on. The best way to accomplish that is to add the right mix of plants, which is often why people choose to have a container water garden in the first place.

What is the right mix? Lilies are not ideal for drawing nutrients out of the water nor do they usually work with many containers. Instead, adding some marginals and/or floating aquatics will help keep nitrate levels down, inhibiting the growth of algae. In addition to plants, you could add bacteria to the water in your container, which will also help consume the nutrients that algae feeds on.

HELP FROM MOTHER NATURE

Fortunately, by creating a mini-ecosystem in your container water garden, you can enlist the services of Mother Nature and all of her friends to help with some of the maintenance.

Can you have a true ecosystem in a container garden? Of course, but you must work with Mother Nature, not against her. So what does it take to create and maintain a small pond ecosystem? Fish, plants, water, bacteria, along with a few snails and insects should just about do it.

Above: Control algae by including plenty of plants to consume excess nutrients. Right: Floating plants like azolla help shade the water, also minimizing algae growth.

GETTING FISHY

In addition, adding some gravel to the bottom of the container, as well as a small fish or two, will serve to speed up the process of your container becoming a natural ecosystem. The nice part about adding fish into this small environment is that you really won't need to feed them. They will have ample food sources to choose from and adding another food to their vast plate will only serve to increase waste production, and ultimately algae growth. One to two small goldfish per container is more than adequate.

It's recommended that you add one snail (quarter sized) for every 20 gallons of water, so it's likely that one snail will do the job in most cases.

You could also "hire" snails to manage that algae growth, and it doesn't cost much ... just their purchase price and all the algae they can eat. It's recommended that you add one snail (quarter sized) for every 20 gallons of water, so it's likely that one snail will do the job in most cases. One problem with snails is that they tend to reproduce quite prolifically. If this happens, don't use chemicals to get rid of them. Just do a clean-out of your container and they will naturally balance themselves.

Feeding fish in a container water garden is not necessary, but it sure can be a lot of fun.

CONTAINER FISH

The addition of fish will help speed the development of your container water garden ecosystem.

Goldfish

Koi

To avoid excess algae growth, be sure to only feed the fish once a day, what they can eat in a few minutes.

MOSQUITO CONTROL

If you're worried about these pesky bugs taking up temporary residence in your container water garden, it is important to take the necessary precautions in the very beginning to make sure they don't show up on your doorstep.

Creating water movement, usually with a small water pump and/or fountain, can help control mosquitoes because they prefer to lay their eggs in stagnant water. This can sometimes be a challenge if the container is not located near an electrical source. Adding a pump or fountain can also add significantly to the overall cost of the container, and if you're on a budget, this option wouldn't be very attractive.

Luckily there are other ways to control the accumulation of mosquito larvae in your container garden. Many have found the gambusia, also known as mosquitofish, to be highly effective in controlling mosquitoes because they absolutely love to eat mosquito larvae and will keep them in check for the entire season. Please remember, though, that these fish are not tolerant of cold water temperatures and will have to be replaced each season. It will take about 5 to 10 mosquitofish to adequately control mosquitoes in an average sized container.

Other options are all natural, microbial larvicide that is designed to kill mosquitoes before they even hatch. This type of product is 100 percent safe for plants and fish and comes in the form of little, floating discs or granules that you sprinkle into the water.

PLANT CARE

Keeping your plants healthy, full, growing, and blooming will go a long way in maintaining a beautiful container water garden. When choosing which plants you'd like for your container water garden, consider what they will look like and how much they will grow after being in the container for a month. Don't overload it with plants... allow room for them to grow. This will cut down on the maintenance you'll need to do as the season progresses.

A – Feeding the Plants

To get the most out of your container water garden, it's best that you feed your plants with aquatic fertilizer tabs (about one tab for every gallon of soil) following the manufacturer's recommended intervals between feeding. Don't use regular fertilizers that aren't meant for plants submersed in water. Doing so may contribute to algae growth in your container. For best results use an aquatic tab that can be inserted an inch or two into the soil.

B – Pruning and Trimming

Pruning is the process of removing parts of a plant in order to train and shape it. Deadheading (removal of dead flowers) and trimming off damaged or dead parts during the growing season will help maintain neat, clean, long-blooming marginal water plants. Doing both of these tasks ensures that the plants stay healthy, and grow and flower often.

C – Watering

While it's kind of funny to think that you might have to water your container water garden, it is actually a necessary maintenance task! During hot weather, you could see as much as an inch of water loss each day due to evaporation. Keeping the water topped off is more for the sake of the aesthetics of the container water garden than the plants. As long as the plant's roots are in water, they will be fine.

In the summer, when you go on vacation, fill the container to its maximum level to ensure that your plants will look good when you get back from a week's vacation.

INSECTS

Aphids are the primary bane of water plants, but luckily they are very easy to control. Watering the leaves regularly will wash the pesky bugs off the leaves, or you can use an aphid spray especially for aquatic plants and safe for fish. This spray is usually garlic-based and repels the insects, but does not kill them. Spray the leaves as recommended by the manufacturer.

In the summer, when you go on vacation, fill the container to its maximum level to ensure that your plants will look good when you get back from a week's vacation.

WINTER CARE – HARDY PLANTS

You should stop fertilizing your plants about six weeks before the first frost. Aquatic plants that are hardy in your area should be allowed to go dormant for the winter. When the cold weather starts turning the plant's leaves from green to yellow or brown, remove them from the decorative container, trim off all the foliage, and follow one of the following processes:

- If you have a pond, place the plants into an area of the pond where the water is at least 24 inches deep. Move plants back into their containers promptly in the spring.
- If you don't have a pond, bury the plants under 6 inches or more of mulch. Again, move the plants back to the container in the spring.
- Put them in your compost pile and buy new plants next year. This isn't much different than the flats of annuals that you might buy each year. Sometimes, it's fun to try new varieties of aquatic plants, and starting over each spring is great way to do this.

To overwinter tropical aquatics, avoid exposing the plants to temperatures lower than 40° F by moving them indoors at the appropriate time for your area.

For what might be considered a semi-hardy marginal in your area, you can take the plants and place them in water (use a bucket or small kiddie pool), in a cool, dark area like a basement. When the weather warms and frost is just a memory, return the plant to its container. If you don't have an area to do this, you could trim the foliage, remove the roots from the tubers, clean them off, and place them in a cool, dry place.

Hardy aquatic plants that have been growing in your container water garden all summer, can be overwintered in your pond.

THE TROPICS

Tropical marginal plants can either be treated as annuals and left to die as the air temperature drops and frost hits them, or they can be brought indoors during these cold periods.

To overwinter tropical aquatics, avoid exposing the plants to temperatures lower than 40° F by moving them indoors at the appropriate time for your area. They can be kept in a watertight container – decorative or not – to replicate the container water garden they were in when outdoors. You can also repot them into a new container, using soil as you would a houseplant. If potted in soil, be sure to water them regularly. Place the plant in a bright sunny window or under a grow light to ensure healthy, robust growth.

IN THE SPRING

In order to get the most out of your hardy plants each season, you will have to keep them growing strong, especially if you re-use them in your container water gardens year after year. Marginal aquatic plants grow fast and furiously and tend to fill up a container, so yearly dividing and repotting is usually necessary. Hardy water lilies should be divided every two or three years depending on the plant container size.

One thing to remember is that aquatic plants are extremely resilient plants that can withstand an early season dividing process with no lasting negative effect on the plant. In fact, it's quite the opposite. Dividing and splitting aquatic plants will give you the fullest, healthiest plants.

DIVIDING MARGINALS

Step 1 – Start dividing your aquatic plants by removing them from the pot.

Step 2 – Using a serrated knife, cut the root ball right down the middle.

Step 3 – Pull the two halves apart with your fingers.

Step 4 – Voilá! You now have two plants ready for potting!

Instead of a green thumb, you can tell your friends that you have a wet thumb!

KEEPING IT BEAUTIFUL

The few steps that are necessary to keep your container water garden looking healthy are really pretty easy. And the payback? They are too many to mention. Don't be afraid to give them a try. Instead of a green thumb, you can tell your friends that you have a wet thumb!

Chapter 6

RESOURCES

AND REFERENCES FOR CONTAINER HOBBYISTS

Can't seem to remember the name of that plant you read about a few chapters ago? Looking for a quick reference for information and inspiration about container water gardens? Well, you've come to the right place! Peruse the following pages for a refresher of information you've learned throughout the book, as well as places where you can find more information on this exciting hobby!

CONTAINERS

Many of the containers used in our projects are offered by the following companies and available at most local garden centers:

Campania, International
www.campaniainternational.com

New England Pottery/Norcal Pottery
www.nepottery.com

Other Container Ideas:

- Terra Cotta Pots
- Concrete or Cast Iron Urns
- Old Sinks, Washtubs, and Bathtubs
- Metal Buckets – Old and New
- Watering Cans
- Assorted Pottery

PLANTS

All the plants in this book were provided by Moerings Waterplant Nursery. Their plants can be found at many water garden retailers. Visit *www.moerings.com* or *www.pondtrend.com* for more information on aquatic plants.

Get creative with a different way of displaying your container water garden.

SPECIAL THANKS

Oscar Warmerdam of Moerings Waterplant Nursery gets his hands wet selecting his favorite plants for our container water gardens.

Jet Dekker, container water garden builder extraordinaire, chooses the best Canna 'Pretoria' for her next project.

CONTAINER WATER GARDEN PLANT GALLERY

Arrowhead
Sagittaria latifolia

ZONE 3 – 11
HEIGHT 24″

Arrow-shaped leaves on massive stems. This makes a great thriller for the container water garden.

Arrowhead, Narrow-leaved
Sagittaria gramineus

ZONE 3 – 9
HEIGHT 12″

Oblong, narrow leaves and tiny white flowers add a delicate touch to the container garden.

Bacopa, Lemon
Bacopa caroliniana

ZONE 7 – 11
HEIGHT 2 – 4″

A great spiller that cascades down the edge of the container. Also works well at the base of taller plants.

Calla Lily
Zantedeschia aethiopica

ZONE 6 – 11
HEIGHT 18″

Tropical looking foliage with a seductive flower.

Canna, Variegated
Canna 'Pretoria'

ZONE 7 – 10
HEIGHT 3 – 4′

Bright orange against purple, variegated leaves make this plant a definite thriller!

Cardinal Flower
Lobelia cardinalis

ZONE 5 – 9
HEIGHT 2 – 3′

Red flowers of this tall growing plants provide a splash of vibrant color to most green aquatics.

Photo by Florida Aquatic Nursery

Cattail, Miniature
Typha minima

ZONE 3 – 12
HEIGHT 12 – 18″

This miniature version of the well-known cattail has tiny, 1-inch, soft catkins on thin, strappy leaves.

Cattail, Variegated
Typha latifolia 'Variegata'

ZONE 4 – 11
HEIGHT 5 – 6′

This thriller of a plant adds brightness to the container water garden. The vertical variegated leaves are white with light green stripes, offering great companionship to others colors.

Creeping Buttercup
Ranunculus repens 'Buttered Popcorn'

ZONE 4 – 9
HEIGHT 8 – 10″

Beautiful green variegated, ruffled foliage and cute, little yellow buttercup flowers make this plant a winner for any container.

Creeping Jenny
Lysimachia nummularia

ZONE 4 – 10
HEIGHT 1 – 3″

The chartreuse, penny-sized leaves of this spiller grow almost anywhere, especially over the edges of the pot. A magnificent plant.

Fiber Optic Grass
Scirpus cernuus

ZONE 5
HEIGHT 10″

A big tuft of grassy foliage topped with tiny brown flowers make the name of this filler obvious!

Forget-Me-Not
Myosotis scorpoides

ZONE 3 – 9
HEIGHT 2 – 6″

Tiny blue flowers with a dot of yellow in the center make this spiller a favorite container water garden addition.

GROWER PICK = *Container Water Garden Favorites*

PLANT GALLERY | CONTAINER WATER GARDEN

Horsetail, Dwarf
Equisetum scirpoides

ZONE 4 – 9
HEIGHT 8″

With classic, horsetail-jointed stems, this mini version works well in small containers where the larger version won't.

Horsetail
Equisetum hyemale

ZONE 4 – 11
HEIGHT 24″

Straight from the dinosaur age, horsetail, with it's interesting, jointed stems, does great in a sunny container water garden.

Iris, Japanese
Iris ensata 'Variegata'

ZONE 5 – 10
HEIGHT 3 – 4′

Sword shaped leaves show off nice, green and white vertical stripes. The flowers are spectacular, but the foliage is what counts most.

Marble Queen
Echinodorus cordifolius 'Marble Queen'

ZONE 7 – 10
HEIGHT 24″

A terrific plant with cool, variegated leaves and runners that cascade over the edges in an attempt to grow little baby plants along the stem.

Marestail
Hippurus vulgaris

ZONE 4
HEIGHT 8 – 12″

Similar to parrots feather, this feathery foliage adds a soft touch as it fills in the bare spots of your container garden.

Marsh Marigold
Caltha palustris

ZONE 3 – 9
HEIGHT 12″

An outstanding filler plant with early yellow blooms that return to greet you every spring.

Papyrus, Dwarf
Cyperus isocladus

ZONE 8 – 10
HEIGHT 24 – 30″

Add a splash of the tropics with this thriller of a plant!

Papyrus, Giant Dwarf
Cyperus percamenthus

ZONE 9 – 10
HEIGHT 12 – 28″

Giant, fluffy papyrus heads adorn the tops of stout stems.

Parrots Feather
Myriophyllum aquatica

ZONE 6 – 10
HEIGHT 6″

Feathery, gray foliage creates a soft mat that spills over the edge of the container.

Parrots Feather, Red-stemmed
Myriophyllum brasiliense

ZONE 5
HEIGHT 8 – 12″

The same feathery foliage and great habit as M. aquatica, but with vibrant red stems.

Pennywort, Variegated
Hydrocotyle sibthorpioides 'Variegata'

ZONE 6 – 10
HEIGHT 1″

Tiny scalloped and light green leaves look as though they've been dipped in white chocolate.

Pickerel Plant
Pontederia cordata

ZONE 3 – 8
HEIGHT 24 – 30″

This filler features lush foliage and bright blue flowers that bloom a long time.

GROWER PICK = *Container Water Garden Favorites*

CONTAINER WATER GARDEN PLANT GALLERY

Rush, Common
Juncus effuses

ZONE 3 – 9
HEIGHT 2′

Tubular leaves spike upward toward the sky.

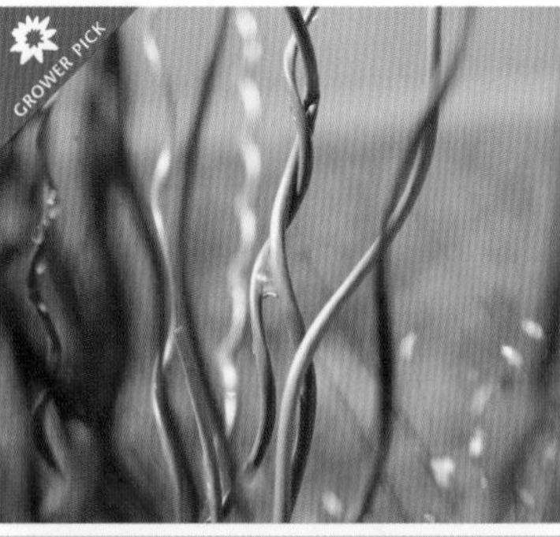

Rush, Spiral
Juncus effuses 'Spiralis'

ZONE 5 – 8
HEIGHT 12 – 18″

A spiller and a thriller with unique, spiraled stems shoot upwards from the center of the plant. An eye catcher to anyone.

Society Garlic
Tulbaghia violacea 'Variegata'

ZONE 5 – 9
HEIGHT 12 – 24″

White and green variegated foliage shoot spikes of pink flowers like fireworks all summer.

Spearwort, Small Creeping
Ranumculus flammula

ZONE 3 – 9
HEIGHT 6 – 8″

Small green leaves are hardly noticed behind the veil of tiny yellow flowers that spill out of the container.

Star Grass
Dichromena colorata

ZONE 8 – 10
HEIGHT 12 – 24″

This plant appears to be flowering all the time with little stars of blooms that float above the plant.

Sweetflag, Dwarf Variegated
Acorus gramineus 'Ogon'

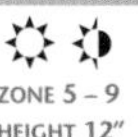

ZONE 5 – 9
HEIGHT 12″

This flexible plant is ideal for container water gardens as it tolerates a range of water depths. A real beauty.

Taro, Black Magic
Colocasia esculenta 'Black Magic'

ZONE 8 – 10
HEIGHT 4 – 5′

Large, elephant ear-shaped leaves on large clumps offer a thriller of a dramatic backdrop to place other contrasting plants against.

Taro, Imperial
Colocasia esculenta 'Imperial'

ZONE 8 – 10
HEIGHT 4 – 5′

Green arrowhead-shaped leaves have a splash of purple in the center.

Taro, Red Stemmed
Colocasia 'Fontenessii'

ZONE 8 – 10
HEIGHT 36″

Glossy green leaves on deep purple stems. Grows a little taller than 'Black Magic' and forms less of a clump. Each leaf is a work of art.

Thalia, Powdery
Thalia dealabata

ZONE 8 – 10
HEIGHT 6′

Gray foliage of the thalia is what counts the most, and the odd angle of the leaves alone are a statement of character and personality.

Thalia, Red-Stemmed
Thalia geniculata f. rumnoides

ZONE 5
HEIGHT 2 – 10′

This plant shows off well by itself, or in combo with others. The bright red stems with contrasting green leaves are awesome.

Photo by Florida Aquatic Nursery

Umbrella Palm, Miniature
Cyperus alternifolius 'Gracilis'

ZONE 9 – 11
HEIGHT 24″

Bursts of green leaves atop 2-foot stems create little umbrellas of green in your container water garden.

 = *Container Water Garden Favorites*

PLANT GALLERY CONTAINER WATER GARDEN

Water Clover, Upright
Marsilea quadrifolia

ZONE 6
HEIGHT 2 – 6″

The softest of green four leaf clovers spreads and spills throughout your container water garden.

Water Hyacinth
Eichhornia crassipes

ZONE 9 – 11
HEIGHT 6″

Indispensable to any water feature, this plant cleans the water while rewarding you with pretty lavender flowers.

Water Lettuce
Pistia stratiotes

ZONE 9 – 11
HEIGHT 8″

Soft and velvety, this floating plant can adorn any space in a container water garden.

Yerba Mansa
Anemopsis californica

ZONE 4 – 10
HEIGHT 6″

White petals surround a white, cone-shaped center. As they age, the flowers get pink spots. Blooms all summer.

HARDY WATER LILIES FOR CONTAINER WATER GARDENS

Photo by Florida Aquatic Nursery

Chrysantha

FLOWER SIZE: 3 – 4″ SPREAD: 2 – 3′
FLOWER COLOR: YELLOW/ORANGE

Comanche

FLOWER SIZE: 3 – 5″ SPREAD: 3 – 5′
FLOWER COLOR: CHANGEABLE YELLOW TO ORANGE

Photo by Florida Aquatic Nursery

Helvola

FLOWER SIZE: 2 – 3″ SPREAD: 2 – 3′
FLOWER COLOR: LIGHT YELLOW

Hermine

FLOWER SIZE: 4 – 5″ SPREAD: 2 – 3′
FLOWER COLOR: WHITE

TROPICAL WATER LILIES FOR CONTAINER WATER GARDENS

Dauben

FLOWER SIZE: 4 – 6″ SPREAD: 3 – 7′
FLOWER COLOR: LIGHT BLUE

Red Flare

FLOWER SIZE: 6 – 10″ SPREAD: 6′
FLOWER COLOR: MAROON

Photo by Florida Aquatic Nursery

Star of Siam

FLOWER SIZE: 4 – 6″ SPREAD: 6′
FLOWER COLOR: BLUE

Panama Pacific

FLOWER SIZE: 5 – 7″ SPREAD: 4 – 6′
FLOWER COLOR: PLUM

GROWER PICK = *Container Water Garden Favorites*

MORE WATER GARDENING

INFORMATION & INSPIRATION

WEBSITES

www.aquascapelifestyles.com
www.aquascapeinc.com
www.pondlifestyles.com
www.moeringsusa.com
www.pondtrend.com
www.nawgs.org

BOOKS & PUBLICATIONS

The Ecosystem Pond
The Pond Guy Publications™
St. Charles, IL
www.aquascapelifestyles.com

This soft-cover book is filled with photos, illustrations, and information on pond construction, fish care, plant care, and seasonal maintenance.
ISBN#0-9753123-0-8

Pond Building for Hobbyists
The Pond Guy Publications™
St. Charles, IL
www.aquascapelifestyles.com

This soft cover book guides the do-it-yourselfer, whether novice or advanced, through a variety of pond installations with photos, diagrams, illustrations, and step-by-step instructions.
ISBN#0-9786506-0-3

The Hobbyist's Guide to Pond Fish
The Pond Guy Publications™
St. Charles, IL
www.aquascapelifestyles.com

The pages of this soft cover book are chock full of photos and information on buying and feeding fish, along with spotting diseases and general care.
ISBN#0-9786506-3-8

The Hobbyist's Guide to Pond Plants
The Pond Guy Publications™
St. Charles, IL
www.aquascapelifestyles.com

Beautiful photos and information on buying, planting, and caring for marginals, lotus, oxygenators, and floating plants are included in the pages of this soft cover book.
ISBN# 0-9786506-2-X

Water Garden Lifestyles
The Pond Guy Publications™
St. Charles, IL
www.aquascapelifestyles.com

Beautiful, hard cover book with captivating photos and inspiring words about the water garden lifestyle.

ISBN# 0-9723214-4-6

Aquascape Lifestyles Magazine
This quarterly magazine covers a wealth of information to guide you through the hobby of water gardening. From fish and plant care to stories about other water gardeners, *Aquascape Lifestyles* proves to be the premier magazine for all levels of water gardeners.

For subscriptions, call 877-206-7035 or visit *www.aquascapelifestyles.com.*

ISSN# 1535-6965

HAWS

Index

A

C

D

F

I